The Transatlantic Slave Trade

Toney Allman

LUCENT BOOKS
A part of Gale, Cengage Learning

GALE
CENGAGE Learning

Detroit • New York • San Francisco • New Haven, Conn • Waterville, Maine • London

LIBRARY OF CONGRESS CATALOGING-IN-PUBLICATION DATA

Allman, Toney.
    The transatlantic slave trade / by Toney Allman.
        p. cm. -- (World history)
    Includes bibliographical references and index.
    ISBN 978-1-4205-0132-2 (hardcover)
    1. Slave trade--Africa--Juvenile literature. I. Title.
    HT1321.A45 2009
    306.3'62096--dc22
                                                    2009008833

Lucent Books
27500 Drake Rd.
Farmington Hills, MI 48331

ISBN-13: 978-1-4205-0132-2
ISBN-10: 1-4205-0132-1

Printed in the United States of America
1 2 3 4 5 6 7 13 12 11 10 09

Contents

Foreword   4

Important Dates of the Transatlantic Slave
Trade Period   6

Introduction:
Centuries of Human Trade   8

Chapter One:
A New Kind of Slavery   10

Chapter Two:
The Infamous Triangular Trade   22

Chapter Three:
Surviving the Middle Passage   33

Chapter Four:
Because of the Slave Trade   45

Chapter Five:
"Am I Not a Man and a Brother?"   58

Chapter Six:
After the Abolition of the Slave Trade   70

Chapter Seven:
Transformed by the Slave Trade   82

Notes   93
For Further Reading   97
Index   99
Picture Credits   103
About the Author   104

Foreword

Each year, on the first day of school, nearly every history teacher faces the task of explaining why his or her students should study history. Many reasons have been given. One is that lessons exist in the past from which contemporary society can benefit and learn. Another is that exploration of the past allows us to see the origins of our customs, ideas, and institutions. Concepts such as democracy, ethnic conflict, or even things as trivial as fashion or mores, have historical roots.

Reasons such as these impress few students, however. If anything, these explanations seem remote and dull to young minds. Yet history is anything but dull. And therein lies what is perhaps the most compelling reason for studying history: History is filled with great stories. The classic themes of literature and drama—love and sacrifice, hatred and revenge, injustice and betrayal, adversity and overcoming adversity—fill the pages of history books, feeding the imagination as well as any of the great works of fiction do.

The story of the Children's Crusade, for example, is one of the most tragic in history. In 1212 Crusader fever hit Europe. A call went out from the pope that all good Christians should journey to Jerusalem to drive out the hated Muslims and return the city to Christian control. Heeding the call, thousands of children made the journey. Parents bravely allowed many children to go, and entire communities were inspired by the faith of these small Crusaders. Unfortunately, many boarded ships captained by slave traders, who enthusiastically sold the children into slavery as soon as they arrived at their destination. Thousands died from disease, exposure, and starvation on the long march across Europe to the Mediterranean Sea. Others perished at sea.

Another story, from a modern and more familiar place, offers a soul-wrenching view of personal humiliation but also the ability to rise above it. Hatsuye Egami was one of 110,000 Japanese Americans sent to internment camps during World War II. "Since yesterday we Japanese have ceased to be human beings," he wrote in his diary. "We are numbers. We are no longer Egamis, but the number 23324. A tag with that number is on every trunk, suitcase and bag. Tags, also, on our breasts." Despite such dehumanizing treatment, most internees worked hard to control their bitterness. They created workable communities inside the camps and demonstrated again and again their loyalty as Americans.

These are but two of the many stories from history that can be found in the pages of the Lucent Books World History series. All World History titles rely on sound research and verifiable evidence, and all give students a clear sense of time, place, and chronology through maps and timelines as well as text.

All titles include a wide range of authoritative perspectives that demonstrate the complexity of historical interpretation and sharpen the reader's critical thinking skills. Formally documented quotations and annotated bibliographies enable students to locate and evaluate sources, often instantaneously via the Internet, and serve as valuable tools for further research and debate.

Finally, Lucent's World History titles present rousing good stories, featuring vivid primary source quotations drawn from unique, sometimes obscure sources such as diaries, public records, and contemporary chronicles. In this way, the voices of participants and witnesses as well as important biographers and historians bring the study of history to life. As we are caught up in the lives of others, we are reminded that we too are characters in the ongoing human saga, and we are better prepared for our own roles.

1444
The first sale of captive African slaves in Europe occurs in Lagos, Portugal.

1510
The transatlantic slave trade begins when a Portuguese ship carries captive Africans to Brazil.

1492
Christopher Columbus makes the first European transatlantic voyage to the New World since the Vikings.

1503
Leonardo da Vinci begins painting the *Mona Lisa*.

1510
Peter Henlein of Nuremberg, Germany, invents the first "portable clock," or watch. He gives it the nickname "Nuremberg egg." It has only an hour hand.

1400   1450   1500   1550   1600   1650

1498
The toothbrush is invented in China.

1664
The Great Plague of London begins. It is bubonic plague, carried by the fleas that live on rats, and it kills more than seventy thousand people before it ends two years later.

1603
Kabuki theater begins in Japan.

1547
Ivan the Terrible declares himself to be czar of all Russia.

1556
The worst earthquake in history hits China and kills more than 830,000 people.

1609
Galileo invents the telescope and observes the moons of Jupiter.

1618
Europe's Thirty Years' War begins in Germany. It is a conflict mainly between Protestants and Catholics.

Transatlantic Slave Trade Period

1712
England puts a tax on soap, declaring that it is a frivolous luxury of the upper classes.

1751
French author Voltaire publishes a book in which he coins the phrase "aliens from outer space."

1777
The slave ship *Hawke* is fitted with copper sheathing, an innovative technology that protected the hull, decreased maintenance, increased speed, and reduced the time of the Middle Passage.

1712
Twelve slaves are executed in New York City for a failed revolt in which nine white people were killed.

1796
Edward Jenner invents and uses the first safe and effective vaccine against smallpox.

1700   1750   1800   1850   1900   1950

1750
The Chinese invade and capture Tibet.

1810
King Kamehameha I establishes the Kingdom of Hawaii, unifying all the islands under one rule.

1841
The first wagon train arrives in California.

1788
The first British convicts are shipped to a penal colony in Botany Bay, Australia.

1855
The U.S. secretary of war, Jefferson Davis, sends a navy ship to northern Africa to buy a herd of camels. The camels are taken to New Mexico territory to carry trade goods and supplies through the desert to California.

1870
The last known voyage of a slave ship to Cuba lands nine hundred people at a port near Havana.

1812
The waltz is introduced as a new dance in England. Most people think it is dirty and disgusting.

Centuries of Human Trade

For more than four hundred years—starting even before Europeans arrived in the Americas—people in Europe traveled to Africa to buy slaves, and people in Africa sold captives into slavery. After the colonization of the Americas began, this relatively small trade in human beings grew exponentially. Between 1492 and 1820, five times as many captive Africans as European settlers arrived in the New World. The Atlantic worlds of Europe, North America, South America, and the Caribbean came to depend on the trade in slaves. Without slave labor and the wealth it generated, they could not progress, tame the wilderness, or prosper. Explains historian Hugh Thomas, "Most of the great enterprises of the first four hundred years of colonization owed much to African slaves."[1] Slavery and the transatlantic trade in slaves were vital to the growth and development of the nations of the New World and, therefore, to Europe as well.

How Could They?

In the modern world it is almost impossible to understand how the buying and selling of people could have been justified, no matter how much labor was needed. Thomas asks, "How was the business tolerated for so long?"[2] Part of the answer is that the transatlantic slave trade was driven by financial and political decisions, not moral considerations. Also, slavery thrived during a time when harshness, brutality, and exploitation were commonplace. The centuries of the slave trade encompass a time when slavery was accepted as a normal part of society throughout much of Africa and in many parts of the world. In Europe these centuries include the fifteenth- and sixteenth-century Spanish Inquisition, when thousands of people were tortured and killed in the name of religion. They include the bloodbath of citizens and royalty that resulted from the eighteenth-century French Revolution. They embrace the period in England when minor crimes such as petty theft were punished by slow, public execution. They were a time when a reformer such as the author Charles Dickens could truthfully write about starving, orphaned children condemned to workhouses and beaten like Oliver Twist for begging for more food. They were also a time when flogging was an acceptable punishment for sailors in European navies.

Paradoxically, the eighteenth-century Age of Enlightenment was a period in European history when educated people embraced reason, moral philosophy, and human rights. Yet somehow, for most people these ideas did not extend to the dark-skinned people of Africa. Even as the United States' founding fathers wrote the Bill of Rights for all people and demanded freedom in the eighteenth century, they accepted slavery and owned slaves themselves. Although a minority of people condemned the idea of buying and enslaving people, the majority of the ruling classes and business magnates embraced it without moral qualms. Slavery and the trade in slaves were impersonal facts of life.

Today the Atlantic slave trade is understood to be a horrifying and outrageous part of history, but it is also recognized by historians as a major factor in the development of the Atlantic world. It was central to the enormous commercial success and political power that are enjoyed by Europe and the United States to this day. For the Africans torn from their homes, it had a huge, far-reaching impact as well. Historian James A. Rawley says that for them, "the slave trade held transcendent importance. It impelled one of the great and little studied population migrations of modern history—the involuntary movement of over eleven million Africans to the New World."[3]

Chapter One

A New Kind of Slavery

In 1562 John Hawkins left the port of Plymouth, England, in command of three small sailing ships bound for the coast of western Africa. His plan was not to engage in exploration or to establish peaceful relations with other cultures. It was to make money. Just a few decades before his voyage, Europeans had discovered the Americas. Already the Portuguese and Spanish had established thriving colonies with large plantations and estates, mining operations, and ranches in the New World. At that time Spain "owned" most of South America and the tropical islands of the Caribbean. One of the most important Spanish colonies was Hispaniola (present-day Dominican Republic and Haiti), and Hawkins had heard that the planters there would pay well for African slaves to labor for them. He had also learned that it was easy to find and capture these slaves along the Guinea coast of western Africa. The Portuguese had been doing so for years. Hawkins and his crews of about one hundred men set out for the Guinea coast and eventually reached the Sierra Leone River. There, says Richard Hakluyt, a writer of the time who recorded Hawkins's stories, he "got into his possession partly by the sworde and partly by other meanes to the number of 300 negroes."[4] Hawkins kidnapped some people by force and actually stole the others from Portuguese ships that were already anchored offshore and loaded for the New World.

A Successful Venture

With his ships fully loaded with African people, Hawkins sailed across the Atlantic Ocean for Hispaniola. He sold the slaves for about one hundred Spanish gold ducats apiece. (No one is sure how much a ducat would be worth today in U.S. dollars. One authority suggests that

Sir John Hawkins was the first English slave trader. He was very successful and became rich as a result. He even designed a crest for himself, which boasted of his conquests.

the price paid for each slave would amount to about $45 today.) Then, according to Hakluyt, he loaded "hides, ginger, sugars, and some quantity of pearls" to carry back to England to sell. He arrived in London after a nine-month journey "with prosperous successe and much gaine to himself."[5]

The voyage was so financially successful that Hawkins reported a 60 percent profit. Even the queen of England, Elizabeth I, was impressed. When Hawkins began planning a second voyage, she became an investor in the enterprise and sent him one of her large sailing ships, *Jesus of Lubeck*, to use in the expedition. Hawkins set out in 1564 with four ships in all and 170 men. Once again on the Guinea coast, Hawkins and his men raided villages and took African people by force. Hakluyt describes the crew "burning and spoiling their townes,"[6] but the crew themselves did not escape unharmed. Seven men were killed in fights with African villagers, and five more were eaten by sharks. Nevertheless, Hawkins eventually captured four hundred people and set sail with them for the New World.

One of the officers under Hawkins, John Sparke, kept a diary of the trip. He wrote about the Atlantic crossing: "Contrary winds and some tornados happened to us very ill. But the Almighty God . . . sent us the ordinary Breeze . . . till we came to an island of the Cannibals [probably one of the islands of the Carib Indians off Hispaniola]." Hawkins sold his slaves, said Sparke, "with great profit, . . . bringing home both gold, silver, pearls, and other jewels great store"[7] worth about fifty thousand ducats (true wealth by sixteenth-century standards). Twenty men had died during the voyage, but Hawkins was rich, and Queen Elizabeth was so pleased with her profit that she knighted Hawkins in gratitude.

Hawkins began the English involvement in the slave trade to the Americas, but he did not start the Atlantic slave trade. At the time of Hawkins's first voyage, European trading in slaves from Africa had been going on for more than one hundred years. It began with Portugal in 1444.

The Beginning of Europe's Slave Trade

Until Portugal's monarch, Prince Henry the Navigator, began the ocean exploration that proved otherwise, European people believed that it was impossible to sail their ships south along the African coast. The further south one sailed, they said, the hotter it became. Sail too far to the south and the ocean would boil, killing everyone aboard the ship. Probably sea monsters lived there, too, they thought. The tales of dangers were daunting, but early in the fifteenth century, Prince Henry's Portuguese sailing ships discovered that they could safely navigate along the western African coast. It was full of life and people. Eventually, Henry's ships made it around the tip of Africa, to the Cape of Good Hope, and up the eastern side. Portugal established itself as a major seafaring and trading power. Portugal's expeditions were a search for wealth, including gold and

The First Transatlantic Slave Voyage

Christopher Columbus actually began the transatlantic slave trade, but it was a reversed trade, and it did not involve Africa. On his second voyage to the New World, Columbus captured five hundred native people to bring back to Queen Isabella as a gift. About two hundred of the Carib Indians died before they made it back to Spain. Says historian James A. Rawley, "In this manner the discoverer of the New World launched the transatlantic slave trade, at first in Indians and from west to east."

James A. Rawley, *The Transatlantic Slave Trade*. New York: Norton, 1981, p. 3.

Christopher Columbus presents the spoils of the New World to the king and queen of Spain, including many native slaves.

spices from Africa and Asia. However, it initiated the trading network in another, even more valuable commodity.

In 1441 one of Henry's ships returned to Portugal with a gift for him—10 captive African people. The exploitation of Africa and the enslavement of its people by Europeans had begun. In 1444, a load of 235 slaves was brought to the town of Lagos and sold to landowners to work in their fields. Prince Henry was there to watch the Africans disembark and was

Prince Henry proved that it was possible to sail south along the African coast. The resulting exploration initiated the European slave trade.

given 46 of the people as his own personal slaves because 20 percent of any venture was his by right. He felt no pity for the captive human beings, but another member of the court did. He was Gomes Eannes de Zurara. He wrote: "What heart could be so hard as not to be pierced with piteous feeling to see that company [the captives]? For some kept their heads low, and their faces bathed in tears, looking upon one another. Others stood groaning . . . crying out loudly. . . . Others struck their faces with the palms of their hands, throwing themselves at full length upon the ground."[8]

Zurara was even sorrier for the slaves as he watched families being torn apart and sold separately to different farms. Few Portuguese, however, shared Zurara's empathy. To them, these non-Christian, dark-skinned people were just commodities to be taken advantage of and used. Within ten years, Henry's fleets of ships had brought several thousand African people back to Portugal to work as slaves in the cities and countryside. The slaves labored on plantations on Portuguese-controlled Atlantic islands off Africa's coast, such as the Azores. Their free labor helped to make Portugal wealthy. Other European nations, which were slowly unifying and beginning explorations themselves, began to eye the lucrative opportunities in trade with Africa.

Slaves for the New World

The world changed forever when Europeans arrived in the Americas and began exploring the continents. It was Queen Isabella I of Spain who funded the first voyages, including those of Christopher Columbus. Spain and Portugal were the countries with the most powerful ocean fleets. They were the first to establish footholds and colonies in the New World. There was so much exploitable land, so much potential for wealth, but there were so few people to do the work of making these colonies pay off for the mother countries. Adventurous and wealthy men could lay claim to great tracts of land, but it was pointless if they could not make use of it. Who would work the fields of crops that could be returned to Europe and enrich the monarchies and themselves? Who would dig the newly discovered precious stones and gold from the mines? To them, slavery was the easy and completely acceptable answer. Almost everywhere in the world, explains the PBS series *Africans in America*, slavery was a common part of life and considered to be "an unavoidable and necessary—perhaps even desirable—fact of existence."[9]

At first the new landowners tried to enslave the indigenous peoples, but Native Americans, or Indians, proved unsuitable for forced labor. With the arrival of Europeans, whole native populations were decimated by new diseases and the unfamiliar arduous labor. This did not prevent the Europeans from seeking out slave labor. Large numbers of laborers were essential to their enterprises, so they turned to other peoples to fill that role.

Slavery as a Way of Life

Slavery has been a part of human societies since ancient times, and most peoples have either enslaved or been enslaved at some point in their history. Slaves worked as servants and laborers in ancient Greece and Rome. They did the agricultural work in ancient China and built the pyramids of Egypt. Throughout Europe during the Dark Ages and into the early Middle Ages, warring groups took captives from each other and made slaves of them. The ancestors of the European peoples—Goths, Angles, Saxons, Normans, Franks, Bretons, and Jews—all engaged in slave

A wall painting from an Egyptian tomb shows slaves at work in this ancient society. Slavery was ingrained in ancient cultures.

trading or were captured as slaves themselves. Later in the Middle Ages, slavery gradually died out in much of northern Europe, but the tradition continued for much longer in southern Europe. Many historians believe that this happened because the Christians and Muslims of southern Europe, the Middle East, and northern Africa continued to war with each other. Taking captives and keeping them as slaves was a way a life.

From the ninth to the nineteenth century, Muslim countries and the highly active Arab slave trade raided Africa for captives and slaves. Experts estimate that between five thousand and twenty thousand people who lived near Africa's Niger River were seized and carried off by Arab slave traders each year during the Middle Ages. The Muslims believed that anyone who did not follow Islam was an infidel who could be enslaved. Both Muslim and Christian societies held that slavery was supported and approved by the Koran and the Bible.

African Slavery

African kings, queens, and chiefs were slaveholders, too. The names of their empires and countries were not the same as they are today. Much of western and central Africa was divided into ministates that were led by a dominant tribe or group, but powerful kingdoms existed, too. There were the kingdom of Kongo (Congo) and its neighbor Ndongo. There were Benin and Sierra Leone. From present-day Senegal in the north of Africa to Angola in the south, both powerful nations and small states had a well-established tradition of keeping slaves when the Portuguese first arrived on Africa's western shores. Describing slavery in one place on the coast of Senegal, a European chronicler of around 1507 wrote: "The gold mines are seven in number. They are shared by seven kings, each of whom has his own. The mines are extremely

Justifying the Slave Trade

Both Christians and Muslims needed a reason to believe enslaving and trading Africans was moral. Some of them decided that it was justified by an Old Testament story. In this story, Noah gets drunk and falls asleep naked in his tent. His son Ham sees Noah's shame and laughs about it to his brothers. When Noah wakes up and finds out what Ham did, he is so angry that he curses Ham's son Canaan. He says that Canaan's descendants will be slaves. In some Christian and Muslim traditions, it is said that all of Ham's descendants were turned black, and so black people were condemned by God to be slaves. Neither the Bible nor the Koran said anything about dark skin, but still people said Africans were the "sons of Ham" and that they were supposed to be slaves. People who disagreed with this logic were ignored. A Muslim writer, Ahmad Baba, argued, "God is too merciful to punish millions of people for the sin of a single individual."[1] Many Christians argued that Ham's story was misinterpreted. Millions of others, however, justified slavery with religion. Historian David Brion Davis says, "No other passage in the Bible has had such a disastrous influence through human history."[2]

1. Quoted in David Brion Davis, *Inhuman Bondage*. New York: Oxford University Press, 2006, p. 63.

2. Davis, *Inhuman Bondage*, p. 64.

deep down in the earth. The kings have slaves they place in the mines. And to whom they give wives they bring with them. Children are born and raised in these mines. The kings provide them as well with food and drink."[10]

Slave ownership was an important part of African culture. In Europe wealth and power were measured by ownership of land, but historians believe that most African cultures were based on a different system. They did not believe in owning land. Wealth and power were based on the size and strength of the kinship group. This was the whole extended family, including people related by blood or marriage. Wealth and power were determined by the number of people a leader could organize, command, and put to work. Slaves became part of the kinship group, although they did not have the same status as true kin. Slaves did not usually come from the kinship group or the nation where they were enslaved. Most often, they were enemy captives, seized during wars with rival kingdoms or tribes. Occasionally, they might be criminals or people punished for breaking religious laws by being sold into slavery. The slaves were dependent on and owed loyalty and labor to the leader of the kinship group.

African kingdoms grew large, and kings and leaders grew powerful by increasing the number of slaves they owned. These people were not exactly part of the family, but they obeyed and depended upon the leader, just as children did. As a matter of fact, in Kongo the word for slave, *nkele*, was the same as the word for *child*.

African slaves worked in mines, cultivated land, served as soldiers, collected the ruler's taxes from people who harvested crops or traded in the markets, waited on families, and occasionally were sacrificial victims in religious rituals. Large groups of slaves were part of the kingdom of Kongo by the end of the sixteenth century. One European report at that time said:

> There are no [free] men who cultivate the ground, nor men who work by the day, nor anyone who is willing to work for a wage. Only slaves labour and serve. Men who are powerful have a great number of slaves whom they have captured in war or whom they have purchased. They conduct business through these slaves by sending them to markets where they buy and sell according to the master's orders.[11]

Trading with the Europeans

When Europeans arrived along the African coast, trading in slaves was easily accepted by both peoples. Although early European ships took some Africans by force, this approach did not last very long. Powerful African nations and tribes successfully fought off European raiders. Peaceful trade between Africans and Europeans became the norm. The Portuguese, for example, established forts and trading posts along the coast of west Africa. One of them was a small offshore island named São Tomé, where the Portuguese maintained friendly relations

An African bargains with a slave trader over the sale of a slave. Africans were willing participants in the selling of slaves to Europeans.

with the Kongo kingdom. The Africans brought slaves there and traded them for European goods.

Both sides in the trade benefited. African leaders were quite willing to trade with the Europeans by selling them slaves. After all, most of the slaves were from enemy tribes and nations, not kinsmen or fellow countrymen. Slavery in Africa, however, was different from European slavery in critical ways. While African slaves could be bought and sold, there were rules about how and when slaves could be transferred. For example, children could not be separated from parents, nor wives from husbands. The slaves were not considered to be mere property. They were captives, but they were human beings with certain rights, and they were often allowed a great deal of freedom. Whole villages of slaves existed who lived their lives without interference except for the duty to grow crops and pay the ruler his or her share. They were more like European peasants than actual slaves. Slaves fought loyally in the armies of their monarchs. They were often assigned positions of responsibility. In many African states, they were allowed one day a week to work for themselves and thus could save up to buy their freedom. When a female slave married a master or gave birth to his child, both she and the child acquired the status of the father and became free people. Many slaves were ordered to do menial and hard labor, but they were rarely cruelly treated.

The New Slavery

The Europeans had a different definition of slavery. Europeans believed in chattel slavery. This meant that enslaved people were property and that they were slaves for life. Any children born to them were also slaves for life. In addition, they were seen as inferior kinds of human beings whose lives were worth little and who

Islam's Slaves

In the ninth century, the Islamic empire was large and powerful. It had whole armies of slaves who fought at the ruler's bidding. These slaves had been kidnapped from Russia, eastern Europe, Persia, Turkey, and Asia, as well as from northern Africa. They were not limited to any particular color. Most of the slave armies were white and were called mamluks. As the centuries passed, Arabs began concentrating more and more on Africa as a source for slaves. North Africa was controlled by Muslims, and Arabs established trading routes from there into Africa's interior. The slaves were then carried off and traded as far away as India and China.

could be harshly treated. They had choices about nothing in their lives.

By the time the Atlantic slave trade began, race became an important part of the European definition of slavery. African people, with their dark skin and "pagan" religions, were seen as little more than beasts to be exploited. Historian Winthrop Jordan once explained, "The English . . . found the African so different . . . that it became increasingly possible for them to consider the African as a different species of human, indeed, subhuman."[12] This attitude was common among most Europeans, not just the English. It made the enslavement of Africans in the New World into a unique form of slavery. It meant societies built upon the use of vast numbers of slaves who could never escape their condition because they were forever identifiable as different and alien. At the same time, it led to societies with an increasing, unending appetite for more slave labor.

During the fifteenth and sixteenth centuries, the Portuguese commanded a monopoly on the importation of African slaves to the New World. However, as Europe expanded its colonization of the New World, other European countries, such as the Dutch, French, and English, embraced the slave trade. In the seventeenth and eighteenth centuries, the slave trade expanded to so large a scale that it was unique to human experience.

Chapter Two

The Infamous Triangular Trade

The slave trade in the Atlantic world formed a triangle of geography and commerce. At one point of the triangle was Europe. It supplied the money and businessmen. The second point was Africa. It had the people and thus the labor. The last point of the triangle was the Americas. They had the land. The combination of money, people, and land led to a commercial revolution in the Atlantic world. It created fabulous wealth for some, radically increased the standard of living for many, and resulted in untold misery for millions of others. The triangular trade (sometimes called the triangle trade) was the route over the ocean navigated by the slaving ships from Europe to Africa (the first leg of the triangle), from Africa to the Americas (the second leg) and then from the Americas back to Europe (the third leg of the triangle).

In the eighteenth century the triangular trade became an essential part of a vast economic system on four continents. The Portuguese and Spanish had dominated the slave trade in the seventeenth century, but now the English, French, and Dutch were the major sea powers. They established New World colonies of their own in both North and South America. They sailed to Spanish and Portuguese colonies and established regular trade with them. They controlled the triangular trade that led to the forced migration of millions of African people to the New World. The slave trade became big business. The British National Maritime Museum describes it as "a triangle of money."[13]

Making the Outward Passage

Although England did not start the slave trade, Britain's National Archives asserts that "they, more than any other nation perfected the system, and, at the height of the trade, carried more Africans than any other maritime nation."[14] The port of Bristol, England, was a good example of a city that depended on the triangular trade. From 1698 to 1807 at least 2,108 slave ships left Bristol bound for Africa on trading voyages. It was here, for instance, that the slave ship *Africa* set sail under Captain George Merrick in 1774. This first leg of the ship's voyage was called the outward passage.

The *Africa* sailed from Bristol to the West African coast on a journey that lasted about six to eight weeks. It was loaded with trade goods for the African market. The goods were carefully selected to appeal to African traders. The cargo of the ship included guns and gunpowder, bolts of cloth, clothing, copper rods and bracelets, glass beads, brass pots, and brandy and rum. It had all been bought by the owners of the ship, who were risking their money on the chance of great profits when the ship had concluded its triangular voyage.

The route that slave ships navigated from Europe to Africa, from Africa to the Americas, and then from the Americas back to Europe is referred to as the triangular trade.

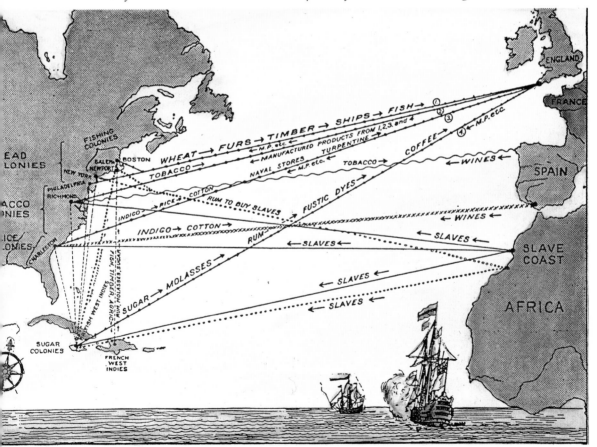

Asientos

The Atlantic slave trade was so lucrative that European governments tried to control who was allowed to conduct the trade. By doing so, they received all the taxes and other monies as their share of the profits. The government of Spain, for example, issued an *asiento*, or contract and license, which gave the bearer a right to sell slaves in the Spanish colonies of the Americas. The first *asiento* was issued in 1595. Pedro Gomez Reynal received the *asiento*, which was supposed to give him a monopoly on the trade. He paid nine hundred thousand ducats for the privilege.

For two centuries the Spanish monarchy gave *asientos* to traders. *Asientos* never worked well in actual practice because traders without contracts sneaked into Spanish colonies or bribed officials to sell their slaves. Once the slaves were in the colony, no planter would reject them; the demand for workers was too high. Spain gave *asientos* to other countries, such as England, but controlling the trade proved impossible. Sometimes, European wars were started over the right to trade in slaves with the Spanish colonies. By the middle of the eighteenth century, there were no more *asientos*. The slave trade was free trade and open to anyone.

The owners of the *Africa*, however, were not the only ones who could profit from its voyage. Before the *Africa* ever left port, there were plenty of profits for the city of Bristol, as there were in every other port in Europe where ships engaged in the triangular trade. The shipbuilding industry made money. The textile industry made money. The merchants who sold the pots and beads for trade in Africa benefited. The companies that made the cannon fitted on the ship for protection made money. The makers of guns and ammunition benefited. The grocers who provided the food and alcohol for the journey grew prosperous. The foundries that forged the manacles, shackles, and chains for the captured people profited. Indeed, some experts say that the innovations and technological discoveries of the Industrial Revolution of the eighteenth century were financed by profits from the triangular trade.

Trading for Slaves

Captain Merrick left port with a well-stocked ship and these written instructions from the investors:

You have a Cargo on board on our Account amounting to £4,648 [equal to about $655,000 today] which you are to Barter for good healthy young Negroes & Ivory, and we desire you'll be very careful in that Purchase of the Negroes not to buy any Old Slaves or Children, but Good Healthy Young Men and Women, and buy all the Ivory you can get.[15]

When the *Africa* arrived on the African coast, Merrick discovered that the ship's owners had guessed wrong about what would be desirable trade goods. African traders rejected most of the glass beads as no longer fashionable. The traders wanted a different size and color, and therefore, many of the beads went unsold. Merrick was unable to trade for as many slaves as he expected. The same thing happened to the *Henrietta Marie* when she set out on her outward passage from London in 1699. The glass beads that the ship carried were not unusual enough to be sought after, but the *Henrietta Marie* carried other merchandise that

Europeans called the trading posts that were situated along the African coast "factories." Pictured here are slave factories maintained by European traders in what is now Nigeria.

did better: Captain John Taylor also carried 33 tons [29.9t] of iron, twelve hundred copper bars, seventy cases of liquor, and many bolts of cloth. These goods were always in demand with the African traders. Other ships often carried cowries as well; these shells were the monetary unit in some areas of the African coast, just as gold was the money in Europe.

During the eighteenth century, ships such as the *Henrietta Marie* might sail for any of the many trading posts or forts that were strung along the African coast or on nearby islands. The Europeans called these places "factories." From north to south, Europeans had named stretches of the African coastline. There were the Guinea Coast, the Ivory Coast, the Gold Coast, and the Slave Coast. Further south were the Congo and Angola. The names reflected the original trading goods available, but by that time slaves could be had everywhere.

African kingdoms and powerful tribes rose and fell during the long history of the triangular trade, but almost always there were rulers, merchants, or just bandits who were ready to deal in slaves when the European ships arrived with their wares. The factories that dotted the coastline changed hands, too, as the European nations warred with each other and wrested control of the prized posts from one another. Gorée Island was one of the thriving factories on the Guinea Coast where slave ships might trade with the ruling Mandingas. Further south the powerful Ashanti might trade at the Elmina castle post. On the Slave Coast lay the harbor of Lagos and the Wydah post on the Bight (or bay) of Benin where, at different times, the Oyo or the tribes of the Dahomey kingdoms ruled and controlled the trade. King Tegesibu of the Dahomey kingdom is an example of the wealth that could be made in Africa at the time of the triangular trade. In one year, 1750, he made more money selling slaves to the Europeans than an English duke could earn over the same period of time. Further along the coast were the lucrative trading ports of Calabar and the island factory São Tomé, where other African merchants willingly traded with the slaving ships.

Captain Taylor of the *Henrietta Marie* headed for Calabar. There, says historian Nigel Tattersfield, "toward the end of January [1700], Taylor loaded about 250 Africans aboard the *Henrietta Marie*—men, women, boys, and girls—all shackled together in the tight, rat-infested, sweltering lower decks. The smaller children, whose wrists were too slender to be held by shackles, were taken to a separate deck where they were piled on top of one another next to a few latrine buckets."[16]

Meeting the Demand for Slaves

Taylor had been unable to acquire as many slaves as he hoped. They were just not available. The availability of captive Africans often varied according to how successful a ruler's war with a neighbor had been or how many raiding parties had gone out seeking people to kidnap. As the eighteenth century progressed, however, and the price paid for slaves increased, some Africans raided deep into central Africa to meet the rising de-

Captive Africans are led by slave traders to the coast to be sold. The demand for African slaves increased as the price paid for slaves increased.

Royal African Company

The English did not begin a regular Atlantic slave trade in Africa until the last half of the seventeenth century. In 1672 English businessmen set up the Royal African Company to establish trading ports along Africa's coast and to sell slaves in the British colonies of the West Indies and North America as well as to the colonies of other nations. The Royal African Company had a charter, or contract, from the king giving it the right to control all English slave trading. The king's charter read, in part: "We hereby for us, our heirs and successors grant unto the same Royal African Company of England . . . that it shall be lawful to . . . set to sea . . . for the buying, selling, bartering and exchanging of . . . gold, silver, Negroes, Slaves, goods, wares and manufactures." The company controlled the British transatlantic trade until free trade became the law in 1707.

Quoted in Hugh Thomas, *The Slave Trade: The Story of the Atlantic Slave Trade, 1440–1870*. New York: Simon & Schuster, 1997, p. 196.

mand. A complex African slave trade developed. At Bonny, for example, near the factory at Calabar, kidnapped people were brought down the rivers from distant villages. In 1789 an English writer reported, "These traders go up [the rivers] in large canoes with two or three principal persons and about forty men in each. . . . There is a mart for trade, where the black traders purchase these slaves of other black traders who bring them down from the interior."[17]

African traders often got their captives by simple kidnapping. An English sailor described a raid in which he participated around 1765. He reported the African raiders "lying in the bushes . . . when they came near a village and taking hold of everyone they could see."[18] Sometimes such captives were shackled and marched for as long as seventy to eighty days to reach the coastal ports where they would be traded to the Europeans. Most of the people sold as slaves, however, were prisoners of war. At times, these wars were directly encouraged by European slave traders who also armed the African kingdoms with guns. In 1712 one delighted member of a slaving expedition wrote, "The battle is expected shortly, after which 'tis hoped the trade will flourish."[19]

Sold, Carried Off, Sold Again

The slaves whom Taylor purchased at Calabar probably had suffered terribly before they were ever offered for sale.

Once in the hands of the African traders, they had to be held in captivity until the slaving ships arrived. Perhaps the conditions were similar to those described at Whydah by John Phillips, the captain of another slave ship named *Hannibal*. He wrote, "Our factory . . . [is] compassed round with a mud-wall about six foot high . . . within which is a large yard [that includes] a trunk [a prison or underground dungeon] for slaves." Any captives who tried to escape were beaten and flogged. But once they were in European hands, their suffering increased. First they were examined by the ship's surgeon or doctor to be sure they were healthy. Then a common practice was to brand the people as ranchers might brand cattle. Phillips, for instance, explained, "Then we mark'd the slaves we had bought in the breast, or shoulder, with a hot iron having the letter of the ship's name on it."[20] Historians believe that the people sold to Taylor were branded "H-M" for the *Henrietta Marie*.

Once examined and branded, the captive people were ready to be loaded onto the slaving ships and to begin the next leg of the ship's journey—the Middle Passage. The Middle Passage was the longest and most dangerous part of the triangular trade. It was the journey from

A white trader examines an African slave to determine his health. It was also common to brand the captives before they were loaded onto slaving ships.

the coast of Africa to the New World and could take months to complete. It was often the deadliest leg of the trip, not only for the Africans, but also for the ships' crews. On the *Henrietta Marie*, for instance, Captain Taylor died of a fever during the Atlantic crossing. The ship was headed for Jamaica to sell its slaves, and its new captain, Thomas Chamberlaine, lost more people before the ship reached its destination. It reached Port Royal, Jamaica, in May with only 190 of the original 250 Africans aboard.

That 60 Africans had died during the Middle Passage did not really concern the new captain. He had lost crew members to accidents and disease, too. He would make a profit for the ship's owners despite his losses. Actually, he had lost fewer Africans than most slave ships. Usually, deaths equaled about 20 percent of both crew members and the Africans trapped in the ships' holds during the Middle Passage. Chamberlaine had seen only 24 percent of his captives die. He still had ninety African men, sixty women, thirty boys, and ten girls. He sold these people at an auction. He earned the most for the men, about eighteen British pounds. He made a bit less for each woman and a few pounds less for each child. The people had been bought in Calabar for less than four British pounds each, so even for the children, he earned at least three times more than they had cost.

Homeward Passage

With his profits, Chamberlaine bought the goods that would make an even greater profit back home in England. He bought bags of cotton and barrels of indigo (the blue dye made from indigo was prized in England). Most important, he bought eighty-one barrels of sugar. Sugar plantations in Jamaica, and indeed throughout the tropical Americas, grew the crop most valued in Europe at the time. Sugar was in high demand, and people grew wealthy by growing, buying, and selling it. Everyone in Europe craved sugar, which grew well in tropical America. Sugar was the reason that Jamaicans bought the African slaves, too. Most would work on the sugar plantations, tending and cutting the cane crop. In other times and places, plantations also grew tobacco, coffee, or rice for export to Europe, but Chamberlaine's load did not include these goods.

The *Henrietta Marie* prepared for the last leg of her triangular voyage. It was called the homeward passage. The successful return to Europe with trade goods from the New World colonies completed the triangular trade that enriched so many Europeans and American colonists. Safe return, however, was not guaranteed. Chamberlaine left Jamaica for England in July 1700, during the height of hurricane season. The ship was caught in a sudden storm about 40 miles (64km) from Key West, Florida. It sank with all its cargo, and there were no survivors.

Many other European ships fared better than the *Henrietta Marie*, despite the 10,000- to 12,000-mile (16,000- to 19,000-km) distance of the triangular trade route and all its dangers. The risks and difficulties were worth it because the profits could be so high. On its first voyage, for example, the *Henrietta Marie* made such a strong profit on the goods it brought back on the homeward passage that the owners were able to finance the second voyage. This was true even though 10 percent of the Africans and half the crew died before the voyage was completed. Some ships reported a 100 percent profit after a triangular voyage, but on the average, owners and investors saw profits of only about 9 or 10 percent. Ships could fail to make a profit because they were lost at sea. They could be attacked by pirates, lose their cargo, and return home empty-handed. During the many wars of the eighteenth century (including the U.S. War of Independence), ships might be raided by the ships of enemy nations.

The Cruel Triangular Trade

A major risk faced on slave ships was also the death of captive Africans. Conditions on ships were so bad that often half the captives died before reaching the New World. The people died of disease, starvation, and beatings and other tor-tures administered by cruel captains. Sometimes, the captives were so determined to resist their fate that they committed suicide. When the trading ship the *Prince of Orange* arrived in St. Christopher (St. Kitts today) in 1737, more than one hundred African men jumped into the sea rather than be sold into slavery. The crew tried to save them, but thirty-three men died. A writer of the time reported that the men "would not endeavour to save themselves, but resolv'd to die, and sunk directly down."[21] There was no profit to be had for the owners of the *Prince of Orange* in those desperate people.

Profits were ruined, too, by the many uprisings that occurred among African captives during the Middle Passage. When the captives attacked the ship's crew, many Africans were killed outright in the attempt to put down the insurrection. Occasionally, the would-be slaves won the battle, killed the crew, and took over the ship. African resistance was a great peril for slave ships, but this did not deter the Europeans. By the end of the eighteenth century, millions of captive people had been successfully sold in the Americas as a result of the triangular trade.

Historians estimate that about eighty thousand Africans were carried across the Atlantic each

A slave is tortured by a ship's captain. Cruel beatings were just one of the perils faced by slaves during the Middle Passage.

year during the height of the triangular trade. The largest numbers—about 40 percent—were taken to Brazil, where they often labored in mines. Most of the rest were sold in the West Indies and the Caribbean islands to work on plantations and serve as domestic servants. About 6 percent were taken to North America, first to the colonies and then to the newly formed United States. These people were the victims of the triangular trade, the survivors of the Middle Passage of the voyage from Africa to the New World. Their experiences came to be defined by that Middle Passage. Writing for the Smithsonian Institution, Colin A. Palmer explains, "The Middle Passage is now synonymous with the travail of enslaved African peoples, the taking of their freedom, their unspeakable suffering, and their capacity to resist and to survive."[22]

Chapter Three

Surviving the Middle Passage

O n Gorée Island, in present-day Senegal, stands a building named the House of Slaves. Captive Africans walked through its back door to board ships for the voyage to the New World. House of Slaves museum curator Joseph Ndiaye says, "We call this door 'the Door of No Return' because African people never returned."[23] As they went through this door, the people forever lost everything they had ever known. They moved into a world where no one spoke their language; they lost their names; often their clothing was stripped from them. Never again would they see their families, their friends, their tribes, or their country. As they boarded the ships, even their humanity was denied—they became chattel, merchandise, or "live cargo." Says historian Hugh Thomas, "Now the darkest time in the life of the slave . . . was about to begin."[24]

The Typical Slave Ship

Almost all slaving ships were specially fitted out to hold as many slaves as possible. This was called "tight packing." Most ships were not large. An average French ship could carry about 400 Africans. A Portuguese ship carried around 370. An English ship usually had room for no more than 230 slaves. A few ships of the time, however, could pack in as many as 1,000. Between the hold and the main deck, slave decks were built that were no more than 5 to 6 feet (1.5 to 1.8m) high. They were made of a series of wooden platforms somewhat like a bookshelf. With manacles, chains, and head rings, the slaves were stowed like books on a shelf, lying sidewise or "spoonways" and shackled to one another, two by two. A diagram of the slave ship *Brookes* out of Liverpool, England, showed a space for each person that measured 5 feet 3 inches (1.6m) high by

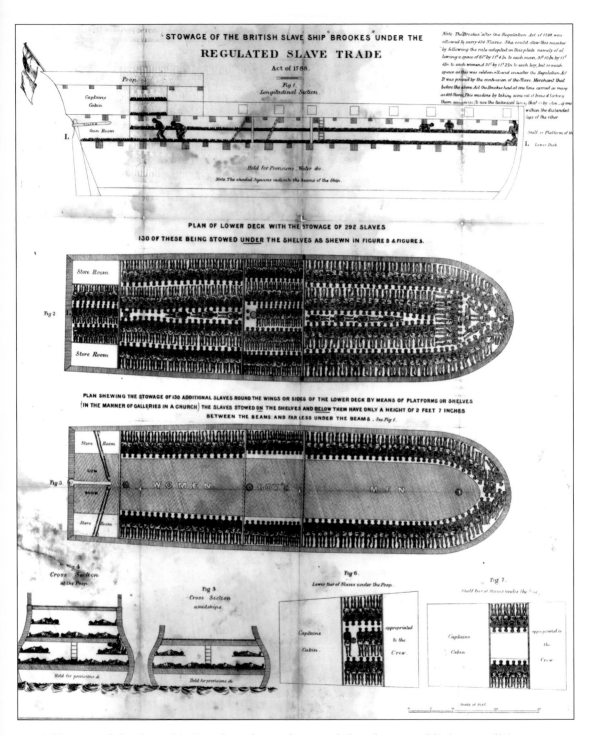

A diagram of the slave ship Brookes *shows the crowded and cramped living conditions that the Africans had to endure.*

4 feet 4 inches (1.3m) wide. In these tiny, cramped spaces, African slaves spent much of the Middle Passage, with almost no room to turn over or shift positions. Thomas Trotter, ship's surgeon on the *Brookes*, described the slaves as often gasping for breath in the hot, packed areas where they lay. He also said, "When stowed in this manner and when the ship had much motion at sea . . . they were often miserably bruised against the deck or against each other."[25]

Packed Onboard

The sight of the slave ship where they were to live during the Atlantic crossing must have filled the Africans with horror and despair. Very few Africans of the time left written records, but a few descriptions do exist that describe the misery of boarding a slave ship. Olaudah Equiano, a child of the Ibo tribe in what is now Nigeria, was captured and sold as a slave when he was a boy of about eleven years old during the 1760s. As an adult, he wrote a book in which he described fainting in terror when he was loaded onto the slave ship because he thought "the white people looked and acted . . . in so savage a manner" that he would be eaten. When he was carried to the slave decks, he was overwhelmed by an awful, sickening smell and the crying and moaning he heard from the captives there. During the time that the ship remained on the coast, Equiano was allowed to come to the upper deck for fresh air, but when the ship set sail, he was chained below with the rest of the slaves. He reported: "The closeness of the place,

and the heat of the climate, added to the number in the ship . . . almost suffocated us. This produced copious perspirations, so that the air soon became unfit for [breathing], from a variety of loathsome smells, and brought on by a sickness among the slaves, of which many died."[26]

Because he was so young, Equiano was allowed to spend much of his time on the main deck in the fresh air after his ship had left sight of land. Most adults on slave ships, however, were unchained only for meals or for the exercise that the slavers believed would keep them healthy enough to survive the trip. Women and children were allowed on deck more often than men, who were seen as dangerous. Even on ships where people were not confined to shelflike platforms, they were crammed into dark, dirty holds as tightly as possible. One ship's surgeon, Isaac Wilson, had the duty of examining the slaves each morning to be sure none were sick or had died. He described taking his shoes off when he went below to check on the people. He did this so that he would not hurt anyone when he stepped on them by mistake. Even then, he had to tiptoe so that he did not step on a slave who had no room to move out of the way.

Horrible Conditions

Most ships in the triangular trade carried a surgeon, and many were paid a commission for each African that arrived alive in the Americas. Keeping the slaves in relatively good health was a valuable economic decision, but it was not a compassionate one. Conditions for African

Slaves are packed in the hold of a slave ship. Being on a slave ship was a miserable experience for Africans.

captives were often violent, brutal, and degrading. Sometimes, captives were so depressed and grieving so much that they preferred death to captivity and tried to starve themselves. This was not allowed. People were flogged and tortured when they would not eat. Equiano tried to refuse food at first. He described himself as so miserable that he preferred death to the slave ship. Two of the crew members tied him up and flogged him. On another slave ship, a French trader, Captain Jean Barbot, described what he did with captives who stopped eating. Claiming to be a "natu-rally compassionate" man, he said, he had to "cause the teeth of those wretches to be broken because they would not open their mouths."[27]

African captives also attempted suicide by throwing themselves overboard, into the sea. These efforts, too, were severely punished. Equiano wanted to throw himself overboard after he was whipped. He wrote: "I would have jumped over the side, but I could not; and, besides, the crew used to watch us very closely who were not chained down to the decks, lest we leap into the water. . . . I have seen some of these poor African prisoners most severely cut for attempting to do so, and hourly whipping for not eating."[28]

Living and Dying as a Captive

Even those captives who tried to stay alive often died of sickness and injuries. By the end of the eighteenth century, most ships could make the Atlantic crossing in about thirty days, but that was under ideal conditions. Storms could delay a ship's passage or force it off course. The trade winds could stop blowing, leaving sailing ships still in the water. If the trip lasted longer than expected, both food and fresh water could run low. On English ships the Africans were usually fed

Where Did They Come From?

Historians can only estimate the origins and numbers of kidnapped Africans. A best estimate of the areas from which the Africans were taken for the Middle Passage, from north to south, comes from historian Hugh Thomas:

Senegambia [Senegal and the Gambia] and Sierra Leone	2,000,000 Africans captured for the Atlantic trade
Windward Coast	250,000
Ivory Coast	250,000
Gold Coast	1,500,000
Slave Coast	2,000,000
Benin to Calabar	2,000,000
Cameroons/Gabon [near São Tomé]	250,000
Loango [south of São Tomé]	750,000
Congo/Angola	3,000,000
Mozambique/Madagascar [East Africa]	1,000,000
Total	13,000,000

Hugh Thomas, *The Slave Trade: The Story of the Atlantic Slave Trade, 1440–1870.* New York: Simon & Schuster, 1997, p. 805.

twice a day. On Dutch ships, they got three meals a day. Common meals included yams, beans, oatmeal, cornmeal, potatoes, rice, palm oil, and a little salted beef. While they ate, they had to be unchained. Crew members were so afraid of revolts and rebellions at this time that they stood over the captives and trained their guns at them while they ate. When food supplies were running low, they were rationed, and captives went hungry. The slave ship *Dorothy* lost all but one hundred of its African captives during a 1709 voyage. The captain explained that there had been "great mortality" because of "povertie for want of provisions."[29] Many times slave buyers in the Caribbean islands complained that the slaves were emaciated and in terrible condition.

Lack of clean drinking water caused even more suffering and death than too little food. A grown man needed a minimum of 1 quart (0.95L) a day, and ships usually stored that much for the journey. However, the water was often dirty, and the decks where the slaves were held were filthy. Sicknesses ran rampant aboard many slaving ships. One of the worst was dysentery, a bacterial infection often caused by dirty water. People sick with dysentery have severe, bloody diarrhea, which dehydrates their bodies. Antibiotics to cure bacterial infections were not available in the eighteenth century, but extra water to reverse the body's water loss would have saved many lives. Unfortunately, the slave ships did not carry extra water. Some historians believe that at least one-third of African deaths during the Middle Passage were caused by dysentery and dehydration.

Another disease that could sweep through the African captives was smallpox. It was a highly contagious, deadly disease that spread rapidly in the crowded conditions of the slave decks. People could and did survive smallpox, but weakened captives were likely to die. In 1713, for example, the trading ship *Oxford* arrived in Jamaica with a much diminished number of slaves. Out of 521 Africans, 95 had survived. An official wrote to the owners in London that "the great mortality was owing to the smallpox which went quite through the ship, not a slave escaping it."[30]

Being Kept "Healthy"

Owners were upset when the captured slaves did not survive the Middle Passage. A Dutch slaving company, for instance, ordered its ships' captains, "Do not permit any Negroes, slaves, or slave women to be defiled or mistreated." It also ordered that the ship's surgeons were to "check the eyes and mouths of the slaves every morning [to be sure they were healthy]."[31] But even those Africans who arrived alive in the New World were subjected to cruelty. On many ships Africans were forced onto the main deck each night for an hour of exercise. Even those who were weak and sick were required to participate. Still shackled in pairs, the slaves were ordered to dance for the crew. If they did not dance fast enough or leap high enough, they were whipped as they danced. The slaves had to pretend to be enjoying themselves or they were whipped again. Since their ankles were chained together during this ordeal, many slaves had their skin rubbed raw by the metal. The crew members of the ships often watched the dancing for entertainment. Sometimes, if they were particularly pleased by an individual's performance, he or she was given a reward of extra food or alcohol.

Cruelty and Rebellion

African captives suffered continual mistreatment during the Middle Passage, both in the filth and darkness of the slave decks and on the main deck. Women were sometimes raped, and men were often required to work and help the crew

Slave traders forced their African captives to dance on deck in order to keep their muscles limber.

Crew members throw mutinous slaves overboard after a failed revolt. Some slaves preferred to die trying to revolt rather than be subjected to a life of slavery.

maintain the ship. People were beaten, mutilated, and humiliated for the slightest resistance. Few accepted their fate meekly. Historians have estimated that there were slave revolts on at least 313 ships during the time of the transatlantic trade. They also point out that 148 ships were lost at sea. Many were probably sunk during storms, but some may have been lost due to further instances of slave rebellions that resulted in the ship's destruction. No one knows the true stories of the ships that never made port.

Ottobah Cugoano took part in one desperate attempt to wreck a slave ship and lived to tell about it. He was about thirteen years old when he was captured and sold to a British slave ship. When he wrote his story, he no longer remembered the name of the African port where he was sold, and he did not give the name of the ship. He did say that it was a British ship that was carrying slaves to the island of Grenada. He said the journey was so "barbarous and cruel" that the slaves decided that "death was more preferable than life." A group of slaves came up with a plan "that we might burn and blow up the ship, and to perish all together in the flames."[32] The attempt failed. The rebellion was put down by the ship's crew, but Cugoano was not killed for his participation in the revolt. In other revolts on other ships, however, Africans were killed by European crews when they attacked. The crews had guns, and the slaves rarely could get their hands on weapons. In 1714, for example, forty Africans were killed on the *Duke of Cambridge* in a failed revolt. In 1722 on the slave ship *Ferriers*, eighty Africans were killed when they tried to take over the ship.

Amazingly, some Europeans could not understand why slaves would revolt at all. William Snelgrave was a captain on several Atlantic slave voyages. He prided himself on being a humane captain. He was sure that Africans revolted only because the crews of some ships were too brutal. He said, "If a commander is himself well-inclined and has good officers . . . the Negroes on board may be easily

"Amazing Grace"

John Newton was a slave ship crewman in the eighteenth century. During one homeward passage in 1748, his ship was hit by a terrible storm. Certain that all was lost, Newton prayed to God to save them, even though he was not a religious man. The ship did survive the storm, and Newton began thinking about turning to God. Even so, he became the captain of a slaving ship and continued to participate in the trade. During further triangular slaving voyages, however, his religious faith grew. He began praying for the slaves he was carrying. Finally, he gave up the slave trade altogether, went home to England, and became a minister. He came to see how cruel and sinful the trade in Africans was. He understood that he had been the lowest kind of wretch to participate in the trade. He wrote a book about the evils of the slave trade. He began to participate in England's abolitionist movement to outlaw the slave trade. He was the slaving captain who went on to write one of the English-speaking world's best-loved hymns—"Amazing Grace."

governed; and many difficulties . . . got over with little trouble." When the Africans rebelled on one of his ships in 1722, Snelgrave was disappointed. He said it must have happened because of "too great kindness to the Negroes."[33]

Voyage's End

"Kindness" was not a part of the Middle Passage. When rebellions failed, the leaders not killed during the uprising might be executed or flogged to death. Whether from violence, disease, or suicide, death was an ever-present threat during the Middle Passage. As just one example, of the 170,642 Africans on ships bound for Rio de Janeiro, Brazil, between 1795 and 1811, 15,587 died before reaching their destination. Those who survived had likely lain in the stinking slave decks for a month or more, surrounded by vomit and diarrhea from their sick companions or from themselves. They had seen the bodies of the dead thrown overboard without ceremony and attacked by the sharks that had learned to follow slave ships. They often had wounds and were almost crippled by muscles that were stiff and sore from being chained in one position for so long. They were traumatized and exhausted.

When the ship came in sight of land, the crew had to try to make these people look healthy and presentable. There was no market in the Americas for sick or dying slaves. The Africans were given extra food to eat. The men's bodies were shaved, and both sexes had their skin oiled so that it would glisten. The ship's surgeon dressed wounds, treated in-juries, and tried to hide scars with ointments. All this activity was incomprehensible to the African captives. They had no idea of what was to come next.

Sold into Slavery

Olaudah Equiano described the terror of the captives when their ship reached port. He told of many planters and traders coming aboard the ship. These people examined the Africans' bodies carefully, spoke strange words, and pointed toward the land. Equiano remembered, "We thought by this we should be eaten by those ugly men . . . and, when soon after we were all put down under the deck again, there was much dread and trembling among us, and nothing but bitter cries to be heard all the night." Finally, he says, "the white people got some old slaves from the land to pacify us [to calm them down and explain in their own language]. They told us we were not to be eaten, but to work, and were soon to go on land, where we should see many of our country people."[34]

At first, the reassurances made the Africans feel better, but when they were carried ashore, they found themselves "all pent up together like so many sheep in a fold, without regard to sex or age."[35] Not long afterward, the people were sold at auction. Equiano said: "On a signal given (as the beat of a drum), the buyers rush at once into the yard . . . and make choice of that parcel [slave] they like best. The noise and clamour . . . and the eagerness . . . increase . . . the apprehensions of the terrified Africans. . . . In this

Slaves for Sale

The following is a typical announcement poster for the auctioning of slaves when a ship reached its New World port:

To be sold . . . on Tuesday the 6th of May . . . a choice cargo of about 250 fine healthy NEGROES, just arrived from the Windward and Rice Coast.–The utmost care has already been taken, and shall be continued, to keep them free from the least danger of being infected with the SMALL-POX, no boat having been on board, and all other communication with people from Charles-Town [Jamaica] prevented.

N.B. [note well] Full one Half of the above Negroes have had the SMALL-POX in their own country.

Quoted in Michael H. Cottman, *The Wreck of the Henrietta Marie.* New York: Harmony, 1999, photo.

TO BE SOLD on board the Ship *Bance-Island*, on tuefday the 6th of *May* next, at *Afhley-Ferry*; a choice cargo of about 250 fine healthy

NEGROES,

juft arrived from the Windward & Rice Coaft. —The utmoft care has already been taken, and fhall be continued, to keep them free from the leaft danger of being infected with the SMALL-POX, no boat having been on board, and all other communication with people from *Charles-Town* prevented.

Auftin, Laurens, & Appleby.

N. B. Full one Half of the above Negroes have had the SMALL-POX in their own Country.

An advertisement for a slave auction. Slavers took care that their slaves looked healthy enough to be sold after enduring the terrible journey from Africa.

manner, without scruple, are relations and friends separated, most of them never to see each other again." Equiano was horrified to see loved ones lose each other because of white men's greed. He wrote, "Why are parents to lose their children, brothers their sisters, or husbands their wives? Surely this is a new refinement in cruelty… [that] aggravates distress, and adds fresh horrors even to the wretchedness of slavery."[36]

The Meaning of the Middle Passage

The experiences of the Africans on Equiano's ship were mirrored for all captives on slave ships no matter where they landed in the New World. It made no difference whether they found themselves in Bridge Town, Barbados; or Rio de Janeiro, Brazil; or Kingston, Jamaica; or Charleston, South Carolina. Those who had survived the Middle Passage and were healthy enough were sold off to the highest bidder. Those who were deathly ill from the voyage were abandoned in their holding pens to die. Newly bought slaves were led off to begin their lives as chattel without a thought to their grief or fears. Hugh Thomas explains that throughout the Americas, "the heart of the matter was the hunger of the colonists for slaves."[37] The colonies and countries of the New World needed forced labor to thrive. And the dreadful Atlantic voyage was part of the price the Africans paid for that hunger.

Today the term "Middle Passage" refers to the entire African experience and suffering during the transatlantic slave trade. It is also a symbol of the strength and endurance of the African people. The captives had to have possessed amazing determination to have survived it at all.

Chapter Four

Because of the Slave Trade

Because of the transatlantic slave trade, entire nations prospered. Planters grew vast acres of cash crops, not because of sophisticated farming machines but because they controlled a labor force that did the work by hand. Mine owners extracted gold and jewels from beneath the earth without facing danger and without struggling to find workers willing to engage in such a dangerous occupation. Families found themselves with leisure time and graceful lifestyles because they had other people to do all their work for them. For entire populations, the dirtiest, hardest, most undesirable jobs were done for them by someone else. The slave trade seemed to many Europeans to be an essential part of their economic growth and power. In the eighteenth century, British trader Malachy Postlethwayt wrote a pamphlet praising the slave trade. He titled it *The African Trade, the Great Pillar and Support of the British Plan-tation Trade in America*. He referred to the slave trade as "the mainspring of the machine which sets every wheel in motion." He added that all of Europe was "creating a magnificent superstructure of American commerce and naval power on an African foundation."[38]

Slave owners in the New World agreed with Postlethwayt. The sugar plantations in the Caribbean were completely dependent on slave labor. In North America, slave labor was essential to the development of the colonies and then the United States. During the height of the Atlantic trade, it was slaves who grew tobacco on Virginia plantations, rice in South Carolina, and cotton throughout the Deep South. Everywhere, slaves worked as domestic servants at the beck and call of their owners. Explains historian John Thornton, "As workers, African slaves and their descendants . . . were a crucial part of the exploited labor force in every Atlantic colony."[39] The slave trade fed the need for labor in the developing New World and met its increasing demand for workers.

The Sugar Plantations

The demand for labor was especially high on the sugar plantations in the Caribbean islands and in Brazil. More than half the slaves in the New World worked on sugar plantations, and life on these plantations was especially brutal. By 1750 plantations in these tropical places were exporting about 200,000 tons (181,437t) of sugar to Europe every year. The planters were growing wealthy, but the slaves who grew the sugar cane and processed the sugar were dying. Throughout the fields, African slaves planted the canes and tended them as they grew. When the canes were ripe, the slaves cut

Slaves work on a sugar plantation. More than half of the slaves that came to the New World labored on sugar plantations.

the ripe stalks with machetes. They hauled loads of cut canes on their backs to the sugar mills. At the mills, slaves ground up the canes to extract the juice. They boiled the juice in huge pots placed over hot fires to evaporate the liquid and get the sugar crystals. All this work occurred in the high heat and humidity of the tropics. And it went on almost twenty-four hours a day.

Michael Cottmann researched the voyage of the *Henrietta Marie* and described the likely destiny of the people sold to the sugar plantations. He says:

> Centuries ago, at harvest time, men and women worked side by side, naked, sweating and bleeding from the lashes of the overseers as they processed cane stalks into the brown . . . sugar.
>
> Sometimes the laborers—who were allowed only four hours of sleep a night and no extra food— died where they worked. The others would be forced to push the bodies of the dead aside and step over the corpses, stinking and covered with flies, to continue their work in the hot sun. . . . The [death] rate among newly arrived Africans was exceptionally high, with estimates of deaths running to 30 percent. Old and new diseases, change of climate and food, and suicide and excessive flogging were the main cause for the deaths.
>
> Plantations . . . were brutal and horrifying. The drill was the same: Enslaved Africans were sent to the

plantations at daybreak and labored all day except for a thirty-minute period for breakfast and a two-hour period at the hottest portion of the day, which was frequently the time set aside for lighter chores.[40]

People worked as long as eighteen hours each day. A priest who visited Barbados, Father Jean-Baptiste Labat, complained: "The English take very little care of their slaves and feed them very badly. The overseers make them work beyond measure and beat them mercilessly for the least fault, and they seem to care less for the life of a Negro than that of a horse."[41] Because of this terrible treatment, African deaths outnumbered births in most Caribbean islands. The natural outcome of this situation was that plantation owners, needing to replace their workforce continually, supported an ever-increasing Atlantic slave trade. More slaves had to be captured in Africa and brought to the New World to take the places of those who had died.

Kindness Is Not Freedom

Olaudah Equiano's fate was more fortunate than a short life on a Barbados sugar plantation. Perhaps because he was so young, no one would buy him at the auction house when he was taken off the slave ship. Along with a few other unsold captives, he was put on another ship and sent to North America to be sold. He was bought as a slave by a rich estate owner in Virginia and separated from all the other Africans. He remembered, "I was now exceedingly miserable . . . [be-

Why Africans?

Some historians believe that African people became the most desired laborers in the tropics because they had a natural resistance to diseases such as malaria. This resistance had developed in their own country after many generations of coping with tropical disease. Natives in America who were stolen from the mainland and carried to malaria-ridden Caribbean islands to be slaves did not have this resistance. The African captives also had a physical endurance that allowed them to cope with the hard labor in the colonies. They often had agricultural skills and experience with handling farm animals in Africa. European colonists and American native peoples usually did not have the same abilities and knowledge.

cause] I had no person to speak to that I could understand."[42]

Equiano was given the name Jacob by his master and used as a house servant. Then he was sold again to a sea captain, given the new name of Gustavus, learned to speak English, and began adjusting to his slave life. Throughout his childhood, he was sold to different merchants and sea captains who treated him well and educated him. After many adventures and ocean travels—including going to war with one master and helping to sell slaves in the West Indies with another—he was allowed by his last owner to save up money to buy his freedom. Freedom had been his greatest wish, despite the kind treatment he had received. When his master told him that buying his freedom was possible, Equiano described it as "a moment of fullest joy" and said his heart was "overpowered with gratitude."[43] He did buy his freedom in 1766 and eventually went to live in England. There he wrote a book about his life so as to persuade people of the evils of the transatlantic slave trade.

A Child's Life

Most Africans who were sold in North America were not as lucky as Equiano. Although their lives were not as terrible or as short as in the tropics, few were treated kindly. About 2 million Africans were brought to North America during the height of the Atlantic slave trade. Venture Smith, for example, was captured in Africa as a young child, survived the Middle Passage, and was sold to a man who lived in Rhode Island sometime during the 1730s. He was used as a house servant during his childhood. As an adult, he wrote a book about those earliest experiences:

I then began to have hard tasks imposed upon me. Some of these were to pound four bushels of ears of corn every night for the poultry, or be rigorously punished. At other seasons of the year, I had to card wool until a very late hour. These tasks I had to perform when I was about nine years old. . . . One day . . . my master's son . . . commanded me very arrogantly to quit my present business and go directly about what he should order me. I replied to him that my master had given me so much to perform that day, and that I must therefore faithfully complete it in that time. He then broke out into a great rage, snatched a pitchfork and went to lay me over the head [with it]; but I . . . defended myself [with another pitchfork] . . . or otherwise he might have murdered me in his outrage. . . . I recovered my temper. . . . He took me to a gallows made for the purpose of hanging cattle on, and suspended me on it. . . . I was released and went to work after hanging on the gallows about an hour.[44]

Olaudah Equiano was an African slave who was educated by his masters and eventually allowed to purchase his freedom.

Condemned by Technology

Until the invention of the cotton gin in 1794 by Eli Whitney, slavery was actually not very popular in North America. The cotton gin made it practical to separate the fibers of the cotton bolls from the many seeds. This, in turn, meant that cotton became usable for making cloth on a wide scale. It could be grown, cleaned easily and cheaply, and sold for cloth making. Suddenly, cotton plantations could be highly profitable. Cotton could be grown on a large scale if plantation owners had the laborers to plant, pick, gin, and bale the cotton. This caused a huge rise in demand for slaves in the United States.

From the time of the invention of the cotton gin, the number of cotton plantations grew explosively throughout the Deep South. Cotton became the most important agricultural product in North America. Over time, plantation owners came to believe that women were better at picking cotton because they were gentler than men when they plucked the cotton boll from the plant. Southern planters began demanding female slaves. Male slaves were bought for the heavier labor. Because of the cotton gin, slavery as an institution spread throughout the American South until its economy depended completely on the slaves.

Slaves working a cotton gin. The cotton gin increased the profitability of cotton plantations and, by extension, the need for slaves.

North American Slavery

Punishments for slaves were often severe and extreme. Harriet Jacobs was born a slave in North Carolina in 1813. In 1860, after she had escaped to the North where slavery was no longer legal, she wrote an autobiography about her experiences. From the time she was twelve years old, Jacobs was a house slave in a family where the master was often cruel, and she also witnessed many cruelties to slaves on neighboring plantations. In her book she wrote about slaves who did not work hard enough in the fields or tried to escape. She said, "The whip is used till the blood flows at his feet; and his stiffened limbs are put in chains, to be dragged in the fields for days and days!"[45]

Jacobs described a neighboring plantation that had six hundred slaves. The master kept both a jail and a whipping post there. She described another master who tied a slave to a tree during one winter night and left him there exposed to the sleet and cold wind for three hours. She told of another slave who was killed for running away after being whipped. Of this incident, she said:

> Nobody asked any questions. He was a slave; and the feeling was that the master had a right to do what he pleased with his own property. And what did he care for the value of a slave? He had hundreds of them. When they had finished their daily toil, they must hurry to eat their little morsels, and be ready to extinguish their pine knots [flames for light] before nine o'clock, when the overseer went [on] his patrol rounds. He entered every cabin, to see that men and their wives had gone to bed together, lest the men, from over-fatigue, should fall asleep in the chimney corner, and remain there till the morning horn called them to their daily task. Women are considered of no value, unless they continually increase their owner's stock. They are put on a par with animals.[46]

In North America owners wanted slaves to have children. Every child born to a slave mother was a slave who could be put to work or sold for profit in the future. Many times, masters were the fathers of the slave children, but still these children were slaves because their mothers were slaves. Unlike in South America and the Caribbean, slave births outnumbered deaths in the American colonies by about 1720. Perhaps this was because the slaves were allowed to live as families more often than on the sugar plantations. Perhaps it was because their labor was not as terrible and long. Perhaps it was because owners saw the value of increasing their "property." But no matter where they lived, slaves suffered and struggled to survive in their new land.

Rebellious Maroons

Throughout the Americas, slave owners commonly used punishment and force to maintain control of their captive workers. In places where African captives outnumbered the European settlers, such as

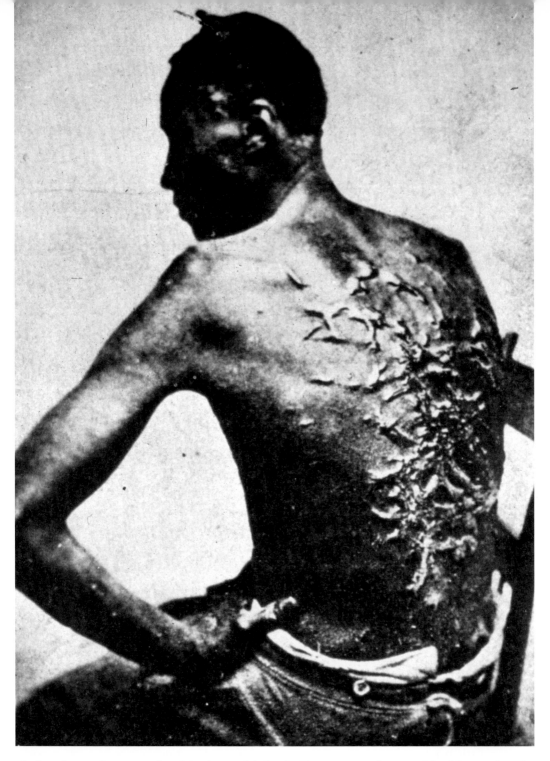

A slave bears the scars of a whipping on his back. Slaves were often punished in cruel and severe ways.

tropical plantations, owners feared their slaves and used brutality to keep them submissive. The tactic often failed. Just as they did on the slave ships, Africans plotted revolt, rebellion, and escape. As a slave named William Grimes wrote, "If it were not for our hopes, our hearts would break."[47] The captives always hoped for freedom and a better life. In North America slave rebellions were not successful, and the people who participated in violent revolts or plots to revolt were put to death. Their numbers were always few in comparison to the Europeans. In tropical America, however, the captives were sometimes able to free themselves.

In Brazil, Jamaica, Louisiana, and other colonies with few European settlers, large communities of Maroons lived free and in defiance of the plantation owners. Maroons were escaped slaves who took to the jungles, the swamps, and the high mountains in order to run their own lives. Usually, they were African-born, direct victims of the Middle Passage, rather than American-born. Many had the advantage of being trained as soldiers in their native Africa. They became fierce warriors who practiced guerrilla warfare against the planters. They raided plantations for food, weapons, and slaves to set free. The planters tried to wipe them out with raids of their own, but some Maroons established small, safe villages and even villages linked into small states that survived for decades.

In Jamaica, the first Maroons escaped when the British fought a war with the Spanish for control of the island in 1655. The British won, but by that time, the Spanish slaves had seized control of a part of Jamaica for themselves. They fought wars with the British who tried to bring them back into slavery. British slaves escaped plantations and joined them. The First Maroon War was led by a powerful Ashanti warrior named Cudjoe and his warrior sister, Nanny. It lasted nine years. By 1739 the English had to face the fact that they could not defeat the Maroons, even with trained English regiments of soldiers. They signed a peace treaty with the Maroons, conceding their right to freedom and control of their land but demanding that they not harbor runaway slaves. There were further conflicts after this treaty was signed. Some Maroon settlements were defeated, but Cudjoe and Nanny's people never lost their independence. Despite having been forced to the New World against their will, they preserved their heritage, their culture, their languages, and their religion.

In St. Domingue (today's Haiti), a slave uprising against the French colonists in 1791 led to independence and freedom for all of the Africans who had been brought there as slaves. The rebellion was a direct result of the terrible treatment of slaves. University professor Bob Corbett says conditions in St. Domingue were "especially cruel" and that the field laborers "were treated much worse than the work animals on the plantation."[48] At the time of the uprising, there were many more slaves than European colonists. Half a million slaves lived in St. Domingue by then, and they outnumbered the Europeans ten

to one. By 1803 the African slaves had driven out the French and set up the Republic of Haiti. It was the only successful slave revolt in the New World, but it inspired slaves everywhere to believe in the possibility of freedom. Haiti became the second independent country in the Americas. The first was the United States, where white people had argued for freedom and independence for themselves while denying it to their slaves.

Freedom Is Not for Everyone

During the Revolutionary War, thousands of slaves ran away from their owners to fight on the side of the British. The British may have owned the ships that carried them to the Americas. The British governors in America may have owned slaves themselves. But, explains historian Simon Schama, the slaves were willing to join their side because "the British were their enemies' enemies."[49] Taking advantage of this fact, the British issued a proclamation in 1775 freeing any slaves who would fight for and help the British army.

The American Declaration of Independence stated that "all men are created equal" and complained of

The slave revolt in Haiti was the most successful of slave uprisings, resulting in freedom for all Africans on the island.

Because of Rhode Island's Slave Trade

In 1756 a little girl was kidnapped in Africa, somewhere between Senegal and Benin. She was loaded onto a slaving ship named the *Hare*. The ship had sailed directly to Africa from Newport, Rhode Island. The captain, Caleb Godfrey, was searching for Africans to buy and carry back to North America. The trip was one of at least nine hundred slaving voyages from Newport, where businessmen saw the profitability of the Atlantic slave trade and decided to send out ships of their own. The *Hare* left Sierra Leone with eighty-four African captives bound for Charleston, South Carolina. The little girl survived the two-and-a-half-month Middle Passage, although sixteen other Africans did not. She was sold to Elias Ball, an owner of a rice plantation in South Carolina. Ball guessed that the child was about ten years old, and he named her Priscilla. No one knows what her true name was or how she coped with slavery. But she lived her entire life on Ball's plantation, married a man named Jeffrey, and had ten children and thirty grandchildren. Her descendants still live in Charleston.

Thomalind Polite is a direct descendant of Priscilla.

America's "enslavement" to England because of unjust taxes. Yet, as Schama says, there was an "embarrassing discrepancy between the rhetoric of liberty and the reality of slavery."[50] John Adams voiced his strong opposition to the British encouragement of runaways. George Washington said the English were traitors to all of humanity for offering freedom to slaves. Patrick Henry saw nothing wrong with owning slaves and yet argued to be given liberty or death for himself.

What to Do?

Haiti's revolution inspired fear and determination in slave owners throughout America. The hypocrisy of the United States brought despair to its enslaved inhabitants. The terrible injustices of slavery began to stir the consciences of many people throughout Europe and the Americas. As the eighteenth century came to a close, the slave trade and its horrors were coming under attack. People began to ask more and more whether they truly wanted to depend upon the cruel slave trade for labor and wealth. One by one, northern states in America started to outlaw slavery. In England, where few Africans were ever used as slaves, the morality of the triangular trade as a source of national income was questioned. According to Schama, enslavement of African Americans was called the "great contradiction," because the same people who championed the cause of liberty depended on the plunder of Africa and supported the Atlantic slave trade.

Chapter Five

"Am I Not a Man and a Brother?"

In September 1781 Captain Luke Collingwood set sail from São Tomé Island on the slave ship *Zong*. He was bound for Jamaica with 440 African captives. The trip did not go well. By November, the ship still had not reached port. A fever raced through the ship. Already it had killed seven crewmen and sixty Africans. Fresh water supplies were running low. Not knowing how long it would be until he docked in Jamaica, Collingwood began to worry about getting enough of his "live cargo" to Jamaica to make a profit. Many of them were so sick that they would be hard to sell to plantation owners, and the sickness was spreading daily. If more of the captives died, the voyage would be a financial disaster. In Liverpool, England, the ship's owners had bought insurance in case there were any losses at sea. Collingwood decided on a plan that would protect them from losing too much

money on his voyage. He would "lose" all the sick slaves at sea. The insurance would not cover "natural wastage" from sickness, but it would cover cargo that the captain claimed he was forced to abandon or jettison at sea. Because insurance would pay for the loss, the ship would not be out the money. And the slaves not yet suffering from the fever would not catch it from the sick ones and would still be salable when they reached port.

Collingwood approached his ship's officers with his plan. He suggested that it was "less cruel to throw the wretches into the sea than to [let them] linger out a few days under the disorder with which they were affected." First officer James Kensal objected that throwing live captives into the sea was "horrid brutality,"[51] but Collingwood ordered it to be done. He chose 132 of the weakest Africans. On November 29, 54 were brought up to the main deck shackled in heavy chains. Men, women, and children were grabbed by the crew at the captain's command and thrown overboard. On November 30, 42 Africans were cast into the sea. On December 1, even though a rainstorm had replenished the water supplies, 36 were tossed screaming and fighting to the sharks that followed the ship. Only one doomed man survived this horrible event. He swam around to the back of the ship and clung to a rope. When he later climbed back aboard, the crew allowed him to live. The *Zong* sailed on to Jamaica and sold its remaining slaves.

Evidence of Inhumanity

The story of the murders on the *Zong* might have stayed secret, except that the insurance company decided to fight the claim of "necessity" in jettisoning the Africans. It did not want to pay the money for the loss to the ship's owners. In 1783 it took the case to court in England. The

Replica of the slave ship Zong. *The* Zong's *captain's callous drowning of sick slaves as part of an insurance scam brought nationwide attention to the inhumanity of slavery.*

jury found in favor of the ship's owners, and the insurance company lost its case. One of the judges admitted that the drownings were shocking but stated that under the law, "the case of slaves was the same as if horses had been thrown overboard."[52] Slaves were considered property, not human beings.

In the court of public opinion, however, the atrocity aboard the *Zong* created a scandal. An anonymous letter describing what happened on the *Zong* was published in the newspaper the *Morning Chronicle and London Advertiser*. Olaudah Equiano was living in London by then and read the letter. He was horrified. He went to visit Granville Sharp, who was a leading British abolitionist (an advocate of outlawing slavery) and asked for his help. Sharp attempted to get Collingwood tried for murder. He failed, but the effort kept the scandal in the public's attention. Revulsion against the slave trade grew even more when newspapers reported that the courts found it legal for owners to kill slaves because they were property.

To Abolish the Slave Trade

Although the majority of English people had always supported the slave trade, a minority had long argued against it, particularly the Society of Friends (Quakers). They were a religious group who believed strongly in peace, equality, and nonviolence. Atrocities such as happened aboard the *Zong* fueled the Quakers' efforts and called attention to their arguments. In May 1787 the Quakers formed an action group named the Committee for the Abolition of the Slave Trade. The original committee consisted of twelve dedicated men. Sharp was not a Quaker, but he became its first president. Another fierce abolitionist, twenty-seven-year-old Thomas Clarkson, joined the group. Their goals were two—to educate the public on the evils of slavery and to pressure the British Parliament to outlaw the trade.

Clarkson's job for the committee was to gather evidence that could be used to persuade people that the slave trade was cruel. He traveled to the ports of England, such as Liverpool and Bristol, from which trading ships began the first leg of the triangular trade. He interviewed sailors about their experiences, sneaked into the slave decks to see conditions for himself, and bought manacles, instruments of torture, and branding irons. With his visual aids and stories, he gave speeches about the evils of the slave trade to sympathetic audiences. The slaving industry hated Clarkson. He received several anonymous death threats and was once mugged and beaten in Liverpool, but he refused to give up. Describing his tireless efforts, he said later, "I lived in hope that every day's labour would furnish me with that knowledge which would bring this evil nearer to its end."[53]

Raising Awareness

As the group campaigned for its cause, members persuaded more and more converts to help them. Clarkson's friend Josiah Wedgwood joined the committee. Wedgwood owned a successful, respected

Women Against the Slave Trade

Although women had little political power in Britain, many joined the crusade to end the slave trade. Hannah More, an English writer, was one of the leaders in England. She wrote antislavery poems, worked with the Committee for the Abolition of the Slave Trade, and became close friends with William Wilberforce. Mary Wollstonecraft was an early supporter of women's rights and another writer who campaigned against

the "inhuman" slave trade. Many middle-class women did what they could, such as boycott slave-grown goods and talk about the evils of the slave trade with anyone who would listen. Later, women campaigners designed a medallion similar to Wedgwood's. This medallion depicted a chained female slave with the inscription AM I NOT A WOMAN AND A SISTER?

Women campaigning against the slave trade made their own version of Josiah Wedgwood's famous slave emancipation medallion.

pottery business, where he produced beautiful vases, candlesticks, and other decorative clay pieces. He decided to help build public awareness by having a medallion designed. It was a cameo of a noble black man, kneeling on one knee and bound in chains. Around the edge was the embossed legend AM I NOT A MAN AND A BROTHER? Thousands of the medallions were made. Women wore them as necklaces, brooches, and hat pins. Men carried snuff boxes adorned with the

cameo. It became a fashion statement that kept the issue of the slave trade in the public eye. Wedgwood sent a shipment of the medallions to Benjamin Franklin in the United States to help raise awareness about the evils of slavery. Franklin accepted them gratefully because he had become strongly opposed to the slave trade. Clarkson remarked, "Fashion, which usually confines itself to worthless things, [is] . . . promoting the cause of justice, humanity and freedom."[54]

Josiah Wedgwood's slave emancipation medallions became a fashion statement that kept the issue of slavery in the public eye.

Clarkson took advantage of another piece of visual proof of the miseries of the slave trade. In 1789 a royal naval captain had visited the Liverpool trading ship *Brookes* in order to see the conditions. He sent a description to Clarkson, who arranged for a detailed sketch to be drawn of how the slaves were made to travel the Middle Passage. The drawing showed the slaves crowded in, the captain explained, "as if they were sardines in a tin."[55] The sketch was copied and widely distributed among the people of England. It made many cry. When he saw the drawing, William Grenville, who would later become prime minister of England, said, "In the passage of the negroes from the coast of Africa, there is a greater portion of human misery condensed within a smaller place than has ever yet been found in any other place on the face of this globe."[56]

Meanwhile, Granville Sharp continued to write pamphlets and articles denouncing the slave trade. He wrote letters to friends in the United States, including political leaders Benjamin Franklin, John Jay, John Adams, and Samuel Hopkins. He urged them to support the American Quaker abolitionist movement and to make the campaign against the slave trade into a transatlantic battle. He began to fight for a free African colony in Sierra Leone where liberated slaves could live in their homeland. One by one, Sharp persuaded most of the Church of England's bishops to support the campaign.

Clarkson circulated petitions among British citizens asking Parliament to make the slave trade illegal. He handed out medallions by the box load. His efforts were remarkably successful. In the city of Manchester, for example, 66 percent of the men signed his petition. In 1789 he sent his brother John to France to discuss abolishing the slave trade in that country. The French Revolution had begun, and both brothers had high hopes that the revolutionary ideals of democracy and equality would extend to liberty for African slaves. Clarkson also talked to members of the British government and successfully enlisted the help of a young Englishman named William Wilberforce.

William Wilberforce's Great Campaign

Wilberforce was a member of the House of Commons. Just as it has today, England had two legislative bodies: the House of Commons and the House of Lords. Wilberforce had influence on both Houses and was friends with the prime minister, William Pitt. Pitt disapproved of the slave trade and discussed the issue with Wilberforce. Clarkson said that at that time Wilberforce "had but little knowledge"[57] of the slave trade, but he talked about the committee with Pitt and agreed to be the voice in Parliament for abolition.

All agreed that it would be best to try to abolish the trade rather than slavery itself. They knew that they had no chance of persuading the British government to outlaw slavery, but they believed that their campaign could force a moral decision to outlaw the trade. They hoped that conditions for the slaves would improve as a result. No more Africans would suffer during the cruel Middle Passage. The planters of the New World would have to treat their slaves better, since they could no longer be replaced by new shiploads of Africans. Torture and killing would stop. Slaves would be allowed to live in families. Their workloads would have to decrease so that they could have healthy children. In the end there would be a slow movement toward free labor, and slavery would die out as an institution.

William Wilberforce took up the cause of abolishing the slave trade before the English Parliament.

In 1789 Wilberforce gave an impassioned speech in the House of Commons, begging for a vote on the abolition of the trade. He spoke particularly about the Middle Passage. In part, he said:

> So much misery condensed in so little room, is more than the human imagination had ever before conceived. I will not accuse the Liverpool merchants: I will allow them, nay, I will believe them to be men of humanity. . . . I verily believe . . . if the wretchedness of any one of the many hundred Negroes stowed in each ship could be brought before their view, and remain within the sight of the African Merchant, that there is no one among them whose heart would bear it. Let any one imagine to himself 6 or 700 of these wretches chained two and two, surrounded with every object that is nauseous and disgusting, diseased, and struggling under every kind of wretchedness! How can we bear to think of such a scene as this? . . . A trade founded in iniquity [wickedness], and carried on as this was, must be abolished, let the policy be what it might,—let the consequences be what they would, I from this time determined that I would never rest till I had effected its abolition.[58]

The Long Fight Begins

Wilberforce failed to get the vote he and the committee wanted so badly. Powerful politicians, merchants, and businessmen testified that abolition of the transatlantic trade would ruin England's economy, hand over the financial benefits of the trade to England's enemies, and bankrupt the planters in England's colonies and lead to their being murdered in slave rebellions. Besides, they claimed, the trade actually benefited Africans. One ship captain explained that the lives of Africans were so terrible in their own countries that they were glad to leave behind the heathen religions, slavery, starvation, and cannibalism of their native lands. He said the slavers were actually doing the Africans a favor. As to the Middle Passage, one witness explained that people would be crazy to think that "men whose profit depended on the health . . . of the African natives would purposely torment and distress them during their voyage."[59] Another asserted that the slave decks smelled sweet with perfume. And one claimed that the captives had such fun with singing and dancing that the Middle Passage was "one of the happiest periods of a Negro's life."[60]

Wilberforce and the abolitionists fought back, but in the end, all they could get was a weak, watered-down bill that restricted the number of Africans that a slave ship could carry and increased the space allotted to each person. The law helped a little, but an unintended result was that even more English ships set sail for Africa to make up for the decrease in "cargo" per ship. It was a setback, but Wilberforce only became more determined. He devoted his life to the cause of the abolition of the slave trade. Over the next ten years, he presented his abolition bill to Parliament almost every year. Every year, it failed, but he earnestly believed that he would someday succeed.

Bitter Failure and Renewed Hope

By the beginning of the nineteenth century, Wilberforce and the committee had little reason for being optimistic. British ships were carrying fifty thousand Africans a year to the Americas. The trade was more profitable than it had ever been. It seemed to be growing like a monster. In 1804 Wilberforce's brother-in-law wrote, "The monster, instead of being cut off, as the first burst of honest indignation promised, has been more fondly nourished than before; and fattened with fuller meals of misery and murder."[61] It was a bitter time for the abolitionists. Napoleon came to power in France, began a war with England, and made the French slave trade legal. The legislators of England would, under no circumstances, consider handing over the profits of the slave trade to their French enemies. In the United States, merchants decided they wanted a piece of the trade for themselves. Rich men invested in European slave ships. American trading ships went to Africa directly to capture slaves to sell in the American tropics, where plantations demanded African labor.

However, there were some positive signs as well. In 1803 Denmark outlawed its tiny slave trade. In the United States,

by 1806 President Thomas Jefferson (although he owned slaves himself) condemned kidnappings of Africans as "violations of human rights."[62] Several states had already abolished slavery and the buying and selling of slaves. Jefferson asked Congress in a speech to outlaw the trade nationally. Finally, in 1804 one of Wilberforce's yearly speeches had an effect. His bill to abolish the trade passed the House of Commons by a vote of 49 to 24. It failed in the House of Lords, but the partial success gave Wilberforce new hope.

Victory

By 1806 new members of Parliament were in power, and many of them were in favor of abolition. Grenville was the new prime minister and a supporter of Wilberforce. Charles James Fox was a new secretary of state, and he was a long-time enemy of the slave trade. Since Napoleon in France was in favor of slavery, many in the public and in government automatically took the other side, saying that Napoleon was a dictator while the English believed in freedom. Abolition became more popular than ever. In 1807 Wilberforce published a book titled *A Letter on the Abolition of the Slave Trade*. In this book he passionately laid out all the moral reasons for abolition that he had advocated over the years. He not only discussed the horrors of the Middle Passage, but also argued that the slave trade was a crime against God and a violation of Christian principles. He warned that "a continued course of wickedness, oppression and

Britain's Shame

Between the years 1791 and 1800, during the height of Wilberforce's campaign to outlaw the slave trade, English slaving ships did more business than they ever had. They carried more than four hundred thousand Africans to the Americas on 1,340 voyages during that time alone. As a consequence the slave population in the British Empire (its colonies) increased by 25 percent. Prime Minister Grenville lamented that England's slave trade would "be remembered for many ages" and called it "inexcusable."

Quoted in Hugh Thomas, *The Slave Trade: The Story of the Atlantic Slave Trade, 1440–1870.* New York: Simon & Schuster, 1997, p. 554.

A painting of a slave ship. English slave ships increased their business between 1791 and 1800 despite the campaign to outlaw the slave trade.

cruelty [will] . . . bring down upon us the heaviest judgments of the Almighty."[63]

The time was right at last. The abolition bill was introduced to Parliament for a final time. Grenville spoke for the bill in the House of Lords. Sir Samuel Romilly gave a speech comparing the characters of Napoleon and Wilberforce. His emotional praise of Wilberforce's long fight for the abolition of the slave trade led to a standing ovation in Parliament. Wilberforce put his head in his hands and cried. The cause that had consumed him for more than twenty years was won. Both Houses voted overwhelmingly to pass the bill. England's slave trade was abolished as of May 1, 1807.

At almost the same time, the U.S. Congress passed a bill making it illegal to import any "person of colour"[64] into the United States as a slave. On March 2, 1807, President Jefferson signed the bill that would outlaw America's participation in the slave trade, a bill that would take effect on January 1, 1808.

Brazil's Great Abolitionist Poet

Every nation had its abolitionists. In the nineteenth century, Castro Alves fought the evils of the slave trade in Brazil by writing poetry condemning its horrors. In his long poem "Slave Ship (Tragedy in the Sea)," he wrote, in part:

Clang of irons . . . snap of whip . . .
Legions of men black as the night
Horrible dancing . . .

Black women, holding to their breasts
Scrawny infants whose black mouths
Are watered by the blood of their mothers . . .

Meantime the captain commands . . .
"Shake out the whip, mariners!
Make them dance more!"

Quoted in *Jornal de Poesia, Agulha—Revista de Cultura*, "Castro Alves, 'The Slave Ship (Tragedy in the Sea).'" www.revista.agulha.nom.br/calves01b.html.

More Work to Do

Both the United States and Britain had outlawed any further exportation of African people as slaves. The United States controlled its state coastlines. England now controlled most of the Atlantic and the Caribbean. It seemed as if the two governments should be able to enforce the ban and prevent slave ships from operating. It seemed that the transatlantic slave trade was truly over. But laws alone were not enough. Abolition of the slave trade did not mean that the slave trade was at an end.

Chapter Six

After the Abolition of the Slave Trade

N ear Calabar in December 1811, Captain Frederic Irby discovered that the Portuguese trading ship *São Joáo* was loaded with slaves. Irby's men boarded the ship, took it over by force, and sent it to Sierra Leone. In Freetown, Sierra Leone, the free colony established by Granville Sharp, the Africans were released. Irby was an officer of the newly formed British West Africa Squadron, a naval fleet charged with enforcing English law against the slave trade. His ship was part of a fleet that patrolled 3,000 miles (4,828km) of the west coast of Africa, ready to seize any ship that broke the law and attempted to carry off slaves. Since Calabar was a British-controlled port, he believed he was within his rights when he seized the Portuguese ship and its slaves.

To Change the Atlantic World

Trading in slaves was now a felony in England. British slaving ships could be confiscated by the government, no slaving activity could occur in any British port, slaving captains could be imprisoned or executed, and captains such as Irby were paid a bonus for each slave they freed. However, even though England abolished its slave trade, slavery was not abolished. As long as it existed, so would the demand for slaves. Britain had the largest, fastest, most powerful navy in the world. The British navy ruled the Atlantic Ocean and used its might to try to control the slave trade. But Britain could not police the world. Britain needed international effort and cooperation to criminalize the slave trade, and that meant that the work of the abolitionists was far from over.

Britain faced three difficult problems in the early years of its determination to stop the Atlantic slave trade. First was Portugal, which had no intention of outlawing its trade and resented having its ships boarded by foreign powers. Portugal and Britain were allies, but Portugal was outraged by the high-handed actions of the British navy. It still owned Brazil, which was heavily dependent on slave labor. Half of Brazil's population in the nineteenth century was slaves. They were needed on sugar and coffee plantations and in the mines. Slave deaths still outnumbered births. According to one British visitor of the time, Brazilian slave owners continued to believe "that it was cheaper to import full-grown slaves than to bring up young ones."[65] Portugal was not about to ruin the economy of its colony.

Spain also resented British interference in its trade. The Spanish Empire continued to include most of South America

The Campeadore *was a Spanish slave ship. Britain's attempt to enforce its abolition of the slave trade angered countries like Spain that still attempted to trade in slaves.*

Abolition

Spain abolished slavery—but not the slave trade—within the country and its colonies in 1811 (with the exception of Cuba, where abolition was strongly opposed and unenforced). Britain abolished slavery throughout its empire in 1833. In 1848 France and Denmark freed the slaves in all their colonies. The United States abolished slavery in 1865. Portugal outlawed slavery in 1869. Abolition of slavery in Cuba occurred in 1886. In 1888 Brazil became the last country in the Americas to abolish slavery.

and parts of North America, such as modern-day Mexico and Texas. In these places, the slave population was small and not crucial to the economy, but Cuba was a different story. The sugar industry had grown explosively, and slaves were its labor force. Neither Spain nor Cuba was interested in abolishing the transatlantic trade. Cuba was the newest, most profitable market for African slaves.

In the United States, only the transatlantic trade had been abolished. Trading in slaves within the country was still completely legal. This meant, for example, that slaves could be loaded on a ship in Virginia to be carried to sales in New Orleans. It also meant that slaves could be smuggled easily from New Orleans to Cuba or elsewhere. In the same way, slaves could be landed in Texas and then smuggled cross-country into slave states such as South Carolina or Georgia. The U.S. government had outlawed the trade but provided no means of enforcing the law. Smuggling was easy and carried little risk. An American ship could sail to

Africa, buy slaves, and then carry them to South America for sale with no chance of being punished. Or a Rhode Island businessman could pretend to sell his ship to someone in Spain, fly the Spanish flag, and then sail to Africa to buy slaves to sell in Brazil or Cuba.

Even though the United States did nothing to stop the trade, it was infuriated by British attempts to stop its ships at sea. Just like Spain or Portugal, it considered any violation of its ships to be piracy and almost an act of war. As a matter of fact, the War of 1812 between the United States and Britain was partially a result of British demands to inspect American trading ships. When the war ended in 1814, the treaty included a statement that both countries agreed "to use their best endeavors"[66] to end the slave trade, but cooperation was limited.

Bending to British Morality

Most seafaring Atlantic trading nations were suspicious of Britain's zeal to end the slave trade. They thought British moral arguments against it were perhaps a way to hide their true motives—that Britain just wanted to control the oceans and prevent other countries from attaining wealth and power. After all, Britain was the greatest slave-trading nation of the eighteenth century. However, Britain's change of heart in the nineteenth century was very real. Says historian Hugh Thomas, the nation "embarked on one of the most moral foreign policies in British history, . . . intended to bring the slave trade to an end on a global scale."[67]

The British government turned to diplomacy. With much persuasion, Spain and Portugal, in a series of treaties, agreed in principle that the slave trade should be abolished. Both countries promised to end the slave trade, but only after a certain number of years, when they had had the opportunity to bring enough slaves to the Americas. In 1815 Portugal also agreed to a treaty making it illegal to capture Africans north of the equator. Britain used the treaty's limits along with the promise of future abolition as an excuse to seize shiploads of slaves as illegal cargo. For the most part acting alone, Britain tried to stop the capturing of Africans by any European or American nation. The abolitionist Duke of Wellington voiced the conscience of the nation when he named the slave trade "the scandal of the civilised world."[68]

The British ship Black Joke *captures the Spanish slave brig* Almirante. *Although many countries agreed in principle to a ban on the slave trade, only Britain took an active role in enforcing the ban.*

As the nineteenth century progressed, Britain slowly began to get grudging assistance from the rest of the world. Portugal and Spain made the slave trade illegal several years after signing their treaties with England. The Dutch agreed to outlaw the slave trade in 1818. In France, after Europe's wars with Napoleon ended and he was removed from power, the French government banned the slave trade. None of these nations, however, did much to stop the trade. It was a ban in name only. Britain continued to claim the right to search suspected slave ships and to push diplomatically for stronger treaties and law enforcement throughout Europe. British ambassadors even went to Africa to try to get treaties with African rulers to stop the sale of slaves.

Progress and Failure

During the 1820s several Latin American nations declared their independence and made slavery itself illegal. There was no longer a slave trade in these countries. They pledged to help Britain in its effort to stamp out the slave trade, but their navies were too small to be of much use. The free nation of Haiti did more. Its constitution declared that any black person who set foot in the country was automatically a citizen. In 1819 the Haitian naval ship *Wilberforce* discovered a Spanish trading ship near its coast that was headed for Cuba. It was loaded with slaves. The captain of the *Wilberforce* boarded the ship by force, unloaded all the Africans, and carried them back to Haiti. Haiti's president, Jean-Pierre

Boyer, declared all the Africans to be free citizens of his country and ignored repeated efforts by Cuba to get back its "property."

In 1823 Brazil declared its independence from Portugal. Subsequently, it signed a treaty with Britain agreeing to outlaw the trade in exchange for recognition of the newly independent country. By 1830 the slave trade was illegal in Brazil. In almost all the countries where African people had been bought and sold, the slave trade was now internationally outlawed. No powerful country except Britain, however, really enforced the ban on the transatlantic trade. Each country devoted but a few ships, if any, to policing its shipping industry or Africa's coastline. A few ships might be seized, but the slave trade as a whole continued more actively than it had before the ban.

Britain continued to push for mutual agreements so that countries could search each other's ships. Its Parliament passed laws basically allowing the British navy to violate the rights of other countries and search and seize their ships. The navy actively sought and captured all the slave ships that could be found. The British instituted a policy of attacking, burning, and destroying African factories where slaves were bought. But Brazil still depended on slave labor, as did the American South, Cuba, and parts of the Caribbean. There was great profit to be made in selling Africans in these areas where slavery was legal. This meant that illegal slave trading prospered.

Voyages During the Transatlantic Slave Trade

Historians have tried to estimate the number of slaving voyages that were undertaken during the four centuries of the transatlantic slave trade, including the illegal era. By country of origin, they are:

Portugal (including some direct voyages originating in Brazil)	30,000
Britain	12,000
France (including the West Indies)	4,200
Spain (including Cuba's direct slave trade)	4,000
Holland	2,000
British North America/ United States of America	1,500
Denmark	250
Other	250
Total	54,200 slave voyages

Hugh Thomas, *The Slave Trade: The Story of the Atlantic Slave Trade, 1440–1870.* New York: Simon & Schuster, 1997, p. 804.

Smuggling Slaves

Wily traders would send two ships to the African coast. One would be slow, old, and worthless. The other would be small, fast, and sleek. The old ship would carry trade goods and money as a decoy for the British West Africa Squadron. The ship might be captured, but it would hold no slaves. The slaves were loaded on the small ship, which sped away while the British were concentrating on the first ship. Other traders abandoned the western coast north of the equator. They went to the southernmost tip of Africa and to east Africa to buy their slaves. In their newly invented steamships, other traders simply outran the older British sailing ships assigned to the West Africa Squadron.

The slave-carrying ships also began flying U.S. flags. The one country that fiercely resisted British seizure of its ships

A portrait of Joseph Cinque, also known as Sengbe Pieh. Sengbe led the successful slave revolt on the Amistad.

was the United States. In order to avoid another war, Britain did not stop American ships as it did other nations' ships. Thousands of slaves were carried to the Americas under U.S. flags.

Once docked in Cuba or Brazil, the captives would be sold with impunity. Trade in slaves when they were on land was not illegal. In Louisiana and in Texas, the pirates Jean and Pierre Lafitte attacked Spanish slaving ships and stole the Africans. Then they brought their captives back to Louisiana, marched them inland, and sold them in Florida or Georgia. Despite the best efforts of the British, slave selling was a great source of wealth. One trader in 1840 said that if he could "save one vessel out of three from capture"[69] by the British, he could make a fortune in the slave trade.

Because they were harder to get, slaves could be sold in the Americas for ten times what they had cost in Africa. Owning the slaves was not a crime because no one could prove (even if they cared) that the slaves had been shipped into the country rather than being born there. Historians estimate that about 2 million Africans were smuggled to the Americas during the period of the illegal Atlantic slave trade. Nevertheless, the British probably prevented at least one million more from being sold into slavery.

The Amistad and the Law

The British did not always have to act completely alone in their fight against the slave trade. In one famous case, both U.S. law and an African prince thwarted a ship and a government involved in the illegal trade. In March 1839 the Spanish ship *Tecora* avoided the British blockade and escaped Sierra Leone with several hundred African captives. One of these captives was a man named Sengbe Pieh, a prince of the Mende people. In June the ship reached Havana. Sengbe and forty-eight other captives were sold to a Spanish planter named Jose Ruiz. Another planter, Pedro Montez, bought four of the children—three girls and one boy. Both of these men lived in Puerto Principe, Cuba, about 300 miles (483km) from Havana. The two men agreed to hire a small ship to take them and their captives to their plantations. They chose the *Amistad*, which had a captain and crew of four, including two slaves.

When the *Amistad* had been at sea for three days, Sengbe found a loose, broken nail. He used it to free himself and all the other captives from their chains and manacles. Then he led a revolt of the captives, who armed themselves with knives that they found in the hold. The rebels killed the captain and one of the slaves. The two white crewmen escaped in a small lifeboat. Two Africans were also killed in the fight, but Sengbe took control of the ship. Ruiz and Montez were at Sengbe's mercy. He kept them hostage and ordered them to sail the ship eastward, toward the rising sun, back to Africa. None of the Africans knew anything about navigation. The Spaniards were able to fool them for two months, until the ship ended up off the coast of New York and was captured by the U.S. Navy.

Sengbe and his fellow Africans were imprisoned in Connecticut when Ruiz and Montez told their story of mutiny. They demanded to be returned to Cuba with their slaves. Was the *Amistad* carrying captives from the outlawed and illegal slave trade? This was the question faced by the American government and its courts. Ruiz claimed that Sengbe's name was Joseph Cinque and that he was legal Cuban property and not just bought off a smuggling ship. Spain demanded that the United States return the Cuban property. Its ambassador wrote to President Martin Van Buren that "no tribunal [court] in the United States has

the right to institute proceedings against, or to impose penalties upon, the subjects of Spain, for crimes committed on board a Spanish vessel, and in the waters of the Spanish territory."[70] Van Buren was not a supporter of abolition. He wanted to give up the Africans, but the courts and public opinion took over.

Abolitionist groups in the United States rallied behind the cause of the Africans and began a two-year fight to save them from slavery or execution for mutiny in Cuba. The abolitionists joined together for the first time in U.S. history. They formed

an Amistad Committee. They found translators through whom Sengbe and the others could tell their side of the story. They hired lawyers to defend the Africans in court. They filed a lawsuit charging that the Africans had been bought illegally, began a publicity campaign, and collected donations to help the cause. When the case was tried in a Connecticut district court, Sengbe testified through the translator, describing his kidnapping and cruel treatment. He leapt to his feet at one point and shouted, "Give us free! Give us free!"[71] The judge found in favor of the captives and said they had been sold and transported in violation of Spanish law. He declared that all the Africans should be set free and returned home. Van Buren, however, ordered the attorney general to appeal the ruling.

The case went to the Supreme Court. The Amistad Committee asked former

Slaves kill Captain Ramon Ferrer during a revolt on the Amistad. *The subsequent trial and exoneration of the captured Africans in America was a significant victory for abolitionists.*

A Boy's Plea

While former president John Quincy Adams was arguing the Amistad *case before the Supreme Court, he received a letter from the only boy among the prisoners, eleven-year-old Kali. Kali had learned English while awaiting trial. He wrote, in part:*

Dear Friend Mr. Adams:

I want to write a letter to you because you love Mendi people, and you talk to the grand court. We want to tell you one thing. Jose Ruiz say we born in Havana, he tell lie. . . . We all born in Mendi. . . .

We want you to ask the Court what we have done wrong. What for Americans keep us in prison? Some people say . . . Mendi people dolt; because we no talk American language. Merica people no talk Mendi language; Merica people dolt? . . .

Some people say Mendi people no got souls. Why we feel bad, [if] we no got souls. . . ?

Dear friend Mr. Adams, you have children, you have friends, you love them, you feel sorry if Mendi people come and carry them all to Africa. We feel bad for our friends, and our friends all feel bad for us. . . . If American people give us free we glad, if they no give us free we sorry. . . . We want you to tell court that Mendi people no want to go back to Havana, we no want to be killed. Dear Friend, we want you to know how we feel. Mendi people think, think, think. . . . Mendi people have got souls. . . . All we want is make us free."

Quoted in Arthur Abraham, "AMISTAD REVOLT—An Historical Legacy of Sierra Leone and the United States," Amistad America. www.amistadamerica.org/content/blogcategory/177/201.

president John Quincy Adams to defend the *Amistad* captives. Adams was seventy-three years old and long retired, and he worried that he would fail. He wrote in his diary that it was almost impossible

to put down the African slave trade. . . . and what can I, upon the verge of my 74th birthday, with a shaken hand, a darkening eye, a drowsy brain, and with my faculties dropping from me one by one as the teeth are dropping from my head— what can I do for the cause of God and man, for the progress of human emancipation, for the suppression of the African slave-trade? Yet my conscience presses me on.[72]

Adams took the case and argued eloquently for the Africans. He said that when they had been captured in American waters, the Africans "were not pirates" but "on a voyage to their native homes." It was their right to take ownership of the ship since they had been kidnapped illegally under Spanish law. The United States had been in the wrong to seize their ship and imprison them. He told the court that he was pleading for "the cause of justice" and "of liberty and life" for his "fellow men."[73] On March 9, 1841, the Supreme Court delivered its verdict and found in favor of the African captives. The international treaties outlawing the slave trade were not just words on paper; they had meaning for these African people. Some of the Africans had died during their time in America, but Sengbe and the rest were freed and returned to Sierra Leone.

Only Freedom Can End the Trade

It was a rare victory for African captives in the nineteenth century, but it had a major impact on the abolitionist movement in the United States. The campaign to abolish slavery gained power, the abolitionists became a driving force in American politics, and the *Amistad* case played a major role in the events that led to the U.S. Civil War and the emancipation of U.S. slaves. In the final years of the nineteenth century, this was what truly ended the transatlantic slave trade—the complete abolition of slavery, one country at a time throughout the Americas.

Chapter Seven

Transformed by the Slave Trade

Without the vast Atlantic slave trade, there could have been no widespread slavery in the New World. Historians estimate that 11 to 13 million Africans were transported to the Americas during the centuries of the slave trade. This number does not include those Africans who died during the Middle Passage. No one is sure how many people were captured and did not survive the Atlantic crossing, but estimates suggest that the total number of Africans taken from their homeland may have been as high as 20 million. It was the largest migration of a people in the history of the world. In every country where the slaves lived, they created new cultures for themselves, altered the development of the country, and enriched the Europeans' culture. Their forced immigration changed the Americas and had a huge impact on Africa as well.

The Impact on the Slave Immigrants

For the millions of Africans who found themselves slaves in the New World, life was forever changed. The impact of their forced removal to the Americas was overwhelming and painful. They had to learn a new language, cope with a new environment, survive brutality and oppression, and somehow still maintain their dignity and humanity and build their own communities and cultures. Generations of the descendants of the African-born captives had to build a cultural identity, even though they would never know their original homeland. They had to deal with the white racism that labeled them an inferior people so as to justify their continued enslavement. The New World was their home, and yet they were alienated and abused in that home. The great African American writer W.E.B. Du Bois lamented, "Why did God make me an outcast and a stranger in mine own house? . . . One ever feels his two-ness—an American, a Negro; two souls . . . in one dark body, whose dogged strength alone keeps it from being torn asunder [apart]."[74]

Africans may have been forced to immigrate, but they did not give up being Africans. Explains historian John Thornton:

Whatever the brutalities of the Middle Passage or slave life, it was not going to cause the African-born to forget their mother language or change their ideas about beauty in design or music; nor would it cause them to abandon [their ideas] of religion or ethics—not on arrival in America, not ever in their lives. . . . Within the space that the slave regime allowed, the Africans re-created an African culture in America, although it was never identical with the one they had left in Africa.[75]

Creating New Loyalties

A neo-African culture developed; it was something neither American nor purely

---

Stolen Roots

The Reverend Curtis Jones is an African American minister who went on a trip to Africa in the 1990s. A little girl approached him and asked where his village was and who his people were. He was stunned and saddened to realize that he could not answer. Because of the slave trade he would never know where he came from or what his roots in Africa were. For almost all African Americans, the links to the past have been lost. Their family history starts with the Middle Passage, and they cannot trace their ancestry back to Africa. Says writer Michael H. Cottman:

We cannot identify a country in West Africa where our individual ancestors were born, let alone a city or a tiny village. We can name only the west coast of the enormous continent.

Where do my ancestors come from? Are my people Ibo, from Nigeria; or Fulani, from Mali; or Wolof, from Senegal; or Ashanti, from Ghana? I may never know.

People often want to know their history and how they came to be, but this knowledge is forever denied to those Africans who were brought to the Americas.

Michael H. Cottman, *The Wreck of the Henrietta Marie.* New York: Harmony, 1999, p. 182.

African but adapted to their new world. In many areas, Africans developed a "nation" among themselves that was built on common language and experience. In Jamaica, for example, the common language and its nation came to be called Coromantee, named after the small village of Koromanti on the Gold Coast. These people spoke Akan, a common language along a wide stretch of the Gold Coast. In Africa the people who spoke Akan might be enemies of one another. They did not even have the same name for the language they spoke. They were members of tribes, villages, and kingdoms, not one nation. In Jamaica, however, the Coromantee nation became the real tie that substituted for the families and kinship groups left behind. Slaves defined themselves as members of the nation and gave their loyalty, friendship, and trust to the other members. They attended each other's weddings, parties, and funerals. They did all they could to help each other in times of trouble.

In St. Domingue, there were three main nations that defined themselves by their religion. The Congo nation was Christian (because the Africans were baptized when they arrived in Haiti). The Senegalese were Muslims. The Ardas were called pagans and heathens by the Europeans because they were snake worshippers. The members of the nations mingled and influenced one another's religions. The new religion, with roots in both Africa and America, was named Voudou by the French. Experts believe that the original African word was *vodu*, which meant "spirit." The Europeans labeled African religions as evil because they were non-Christian. "Voudou" came to be spelled "Voodoo" and was labeled by Europeans as the practice of sorcery and black magic. For the Africans of Haiti, however, it was a true religion, practiced in secret so that they would not be punished by plantation owners. It combined elements of Christianity, paganism, and Islam to form a belief system unique to the Americas.

In 1791 a Voudou ceremony, led by an African priest named Boukman, inspired the participants to fight for freedom and helped to begin the Haitian revolution. Tradition says that Boukman prayed:

The god who created the earth; who created the sun that gives us light. The god who holds up the ocean; who makes the thunder roar. Our God who has ears to hear. You who are hidden in the clouds; who watch us from where you are. You see all that the white has made us suffer. The white man's god asks him to commit crimes. But the god within us wants to do good. Our god, who is so good, so just, He orders us to revenge our wrongs. It's He who will direct our arms and bring us the victory. It's He who will assist us. We all should throw away the image of the white men's god who is so pitiless. Listen to the voice for liberty that sings in all our hearts.[76]

Hidden Culture

African religions in the Americas adapted to the terrible circumstances of slavery. Art forms, music, and social or-

Two men demonstrate the martial art of capoeira. Brazilian slaves developed capoeira as a method of fighting disguised as dancing.

ganization were transformed as well. Slaves often had to hide their efforts to maintain their culture. In Brazil, any attempt to form a community was brutally discouraged by the plantation owners. Because there were so many slaves in Brazil, says historian John Thornton, the Europeans were "concerned to the point of paranoia about . . . group activities."[77] So the slaves had to make their activities appear harmless. Capoeira is a martial art developed by the Africans in Brazil. Latin American researcher Jihan Abdalla explains that legends say "the slaves invented *capoeira* as a fight, but disguised it as a dance so that the white slave own-

ers wouldn't realize what was going on."[78] Capoeira became a kind of dance or game that taught alertness, self-confidence, and the ability to fight hand-to-hand. It became a cultural expression unique to Brazil with roots in African warrior training.

Sorrow Songs

In the United States, Africans often accepted Christianity and usually lived too far apart from one another to form nations. Instead, the plantation became the focus of their community. When possible, they also formed friendships with people on nearby plantations. If family

Slaves sang "sorrow songs" as a way of maintaining community and cultural ties.

members lived on those other plantations, they fought to maintain ties with them. Music and stories became ways that the people expressed their grief and pain and kept their memories and traditions alive. W.E.B. Du Bois called the African American music created by slaves the "Sorrow Songs."[79]

Du Bois says that through sorrow songs, "the soul of the black slave spoke to men."[80] They were a blend of African and American sounds and ideas that became the unique "spiritual heritage of the nation and the greatest gift of the Negro people."[81] They were a North American art form that influenced the entire U.S. culture.

African American religious songs and spirituals were heard and enjoyed in the white culture. Historian Gerald Early calls the spirituals "the most highly regarded black musical expression ever invented in the United States."[82] Sometimes, these songs also had a double meaning in slave culture, beyond what plantation owners understood. Slaves adapted to the demands of slavery by hiding secret codes in their songs. Most historians believe that the lyrics of some songs were used to arrange a secret meeting or even to warn of an escape attempt. For example, a song about fleeing Earthly life for heaven might refer not to religion but to a plan for running away.

Saving Memories

Africans in America found ways, too, to pass on their memories and heritage to children and grandchildren. Their oral histories ensured that their descendants would not forget their roots or the trials that the Africans had endured. One elderly slave in the United States was able to repeat a story told to him by his grandfather about the Middle Passage. He remembered:

> By 'n by de wind calm down. Folks got well
>
> an' started eatin'. So dey lets all but de mean
>
> ones come up on deck. Den dey sings. One sings,
>
> an' de res' hum lak. What dey sing?
>
> Nobody don' know. Dey sing language what
>
> Dey learn in Africa when dey was free![83]

Stories helped African American children to remember that their people were not always slaves and that they had a history of their own. They are still almost the only history available of the trials of the people who were the victims of the Atlantic slave trade.

Traditional African legends were passed on, too. The stories evolved to suit the New World and its language. An English planter in Jamaica wrote about a slave woman named Vine who was a beloved storyteller. She was Coromantee, but she told her stories in English be-

cause the white people wanted to listen. The African folktales of Anansi, a clever, tricky spider, became stories about Nancy the spider. In such ways African culture became a part of American culture, even among the Europeans. In time and throughout the Americas, explains the Smithsonian Institution, "the larger societies in which slaves lived became infused with African heritage."[84]

African immigrants, through their forced labor, were responsible for building the New World. They cleared the forests, plowed the fields, reaped the crops, and built the cities. They also adapted to and changed their new lands and had a huge impact on the art, music, religion, and culture of the Americas. At the same time, the slave trade devastated Africa.

The Impact on Africa

During the height of the transatlantic slave trade, Africa lost millions of young people forever. Experts still try to understand the effect this loss had on the development of the continent. Hugh Thomas says, "The impact on West Africa was, of course, colossal, but it is not easy to give an impression of the consequences so far."[85] A big part of the problem is that no one knows what the population of Africa was at the time of the slave trade. Even the number of people lost to Africa because of the slave trade can only be estimated. However, many historians point out that the people taken from Africa were likely the strongest, healthiest, and most capable. They were the younger generations upon whom the future of all societies depends. They were the people most desired as slaves in the Americas, and they were the people who would have made the biggest contributions to their native societies. Their skills, talents, and creativity were lost to their homeland. Perhaps this made it much more difficult for African countries to progress and develop. Many of the young and most energetic people had been stolen away.

The constant raiding and wars to capture slaves decimated whole populations in Africa. The warlords of kingdoms such as the Ashanti and Dahomey kept only young adults and children to sell for slaves. Babies and old people, explains historian Paul E. Lovejoy, "were deliberately killed as undesirable captives."[86] Even when "undesirable" people survived, they often faced famine. There was no one left to hunt or plant and harvest the crops. If

An illustration of captured Africans preparing to board slave ships. Historians estimate that the forced emigration of so many Africans had a devastating impact on development in Africa.

A Home for Freed Americans

As abolitionists in America gained influence, many white people in America worried about what would happen if slaves gained their freedom. Some owners had freed their slaves, and these African Americans were living independently. Some people worried that free Africans in the United States would encourage rebellion in their slaves. Some people worried that the freed people would be kidnapped and sold back into slavery. Others thought the freed slaves had a right to return to their homeland.

A group of citizens, including the statesmen John Randolph and Henry Clay, founded the American Colonization Society. Its plan was to establish a free colony in Africa for America's freed slaves. The colony was named Liberia. The first group of eighty-eight colonists sailed to Liberia in 1821. The American Colonization Society had bought their freedom so that they could emigrate. For decades, even after the Civil War, thousands of freed Africans immigrated to Liberia. Many had been born in the United States and had a terrible time adjusting to their new land. Nevertheless, the country was able to declare its independence in 1847. Liberia is the only country in Africa established because of the transatlantic homeward passage of freed slaves.

An artist shows freed slaves arriving in Liberia. The American Colonization Society sponsored the founding of Liberia as an African homeland for liberated slaves.

the people did not die of starvation, they often died from disease because they were weakened by a poor diet. The wars and raids frightened other societies so much that whole tribes abandoned their homes and fled far from the slaving routes into jungles or mountains. These people lived precarious lives. Instead of concentrating on improving their societies, farming, and gathering wealth, they had to concentrate on hiding and defending themselves.

As the slave trade reached its peak in the eighteenth century, European traders did their best to encourage wars among African kingdoms. They encouraged one ruler to attack another. They gave advice and guns to help the favored ruler win his war. They promised riches in return for slaves. This often meant that greedy, corrupt people (who did not mind cooperating and ruthlessly preying on other people) became the rulers. They were the ones with the guns and the money to take over. The kingdoms that cooperated with the Europeans were strengthened and grew powerful. Other kingdoms, needing to protect themselves, joined in the slave trade in order to gain wealth and guns for themselves. One Dutch slave trader wrote about the Gold Coast in 1705, "[It] has already changed into a Slave Coast, and . . . nowadays the natives no longer occupy themselves with the search for gold, but rather make war on each other to furnish slaves."[87] Sometimes, according to historian John Thornton, traders even resorted to bribing a ruler to persuade him to go to war and capture slaves. Often the armies were slave armies, and many soldiers died as a result of the constant wars.

In the end, the combination of famine, disease, war deaths, and the Atlantic slave trade led to a failure of population growth in Africa. The Applied History Research Group of the University of Calgary says:

> It has been estimated that in 1600, the population of Africa stood at about 50 million people, or thirty per cent of the combined populations of the New World, Europe, the Middle East, and Africa. By 1900 the population of Africa had grown to 70 million, but made up only ten per cent of the total combined population. Furthermore, the population of Africa in 1850 has been estimated to have been only about half of what it would have been had slavery and the slave trade not been a factor in African history.[88]

In other words, the populations of most of the Atlantic world grew rapidly throughout the height of the Atlantic slave trade, but the population of Africa did not. Its percentage of the population fell in comparison to other continents. This stagnation in population was destructive to Africa. Without people, it could not make social progress or even defend itself. Many historians believe that the slave trade disrupted Africa so much that European powers could easily conquer most regions of Africa. African colonialism was the result. After the slave trade ended, European countries took over Africa and claimed colonies for themselves that divided up

Gullah Culture

On the Sea Islands off the coastlines of Georgia and South Carolina live the descendants of African slaves who developed a unique culture in America. The original immigrants came from different parts of Africa, but over time, their traditions and languages blended and became one culture known as Gullah (perhaps named for Angola). At first the Africans were slaves on rice plantations. After the abolition of slavery, the isolated islands were abandoned altogether by white people. The African American people were able to keep their own traditions and develop their culture undisturbed by outsiders. This culture combined traditions, languages, and art forms that originated in Africa but changed to suit their new society. The people continue, for example, to weave baskets and make clay pots and musical instruments as their ancestors did in Africa. Their songs include phrases of Mende, and their stories are of African origin. Their language is a unique blend of African languages and English. Their music is both African and American. Many Gullah people can still trace their ancestors back to specific tribes in Africa because of the oral histories told by their ancestors.

The Georgia Sea Island Singers are part of the unique Gullah culture.

the continent. In large part as a result of the effects of the slave trade on kingdoms and population growth, the peoples of Africa lost their independence and their right to control their lives.

A Lasting Legacy

While other regions of the world underwent industrial revolutions, technological advances, and the building of great empires, Africa remained fragmented and poor. Today Joseph Ndiaye in Senegal admits that Africa remains underdeveloped in comparison to much of the world. He points out, however, that people must

talk honestly about why it is so underdeveloped.

It is because white Europeans came to Africa and enslaved African people; Europeans took the best of what Africa had to offer, stripped us of our strongest people, depleted our resources, disrupted our civilization, and separated us from our families.

Our holocaust was the biggest crime against humanity. They can continue to call us an underdeveloped continent. The reasons that Africa is underdeveloped are very clear to us and should be clear to anyone who reviews history honestly.[89]

Many in Africa refer to the Atlantic slave trade as Africa's "Maafa," which means "great disaster" in Swahili. Others call it the African Diaspora, meaning the scattering of the people from their homeland. Ndiaye calls it a holocaust, but whatever words are used, it was a tragedy for Africa. It was the most highly organized, largest, and most dehumanizing form of slavery ever practiced in the history of the Atlantic world. When the slave trade ended, the African kingdoms built upon it collapsed, leaving the continent even more vulnerable to European takeover.

For the people who were victims of the slave trade, the difficulties and pain can only be imagined. Historian John Henrik Clarke explains:

The drama of African survival in what is called the new world went beyond drama itself. In conditions that defied human imagination, for a protracted period lasting over three hundred years, Africans, using various techniques, pretenses, and acts of both submission and rebellion, went beyond survival and prevailed in order to live and still be a people in spite of the massive effort to destroy every aspect of their humanity.[90]

That the Africans prevailed and thrived was the Americas' great blessing. Thinkquest's "Trade Links" Web site says that it led "to a cultural diversity unseen in world history."[91] It transformed the New World.

Notes

Introduction: Centuries of Human Trade

1. Hugh Thomas, *The Slave Trade*. New York: Simon & Schuster, 1997, p. 793.
2. Thomas, *The Slave Trade*, p. 14.
3. James A. Rawley, *The Transatlantic Slave Trade*. New York: Norton, 1981, p. 5.

Chapter One: A New Kind of Slavery

4. Quoted in Black Presence, British National Archives, "Adventurers and Slavers: Early Times." www.national archives.gov.uk/pathways/blackhist ory/early_times/adventurers.htm.
5. Quoted in Thomas, *The Slave Trade*, p. 157.
6. Quoted in Thomas, *The Slave Trade*, p. 157.
7. Quoted in William Wood, *Elizabethan Sea Dogs*. New Haven, CT: Yale University Press, 1918: eBook. www.full books.com/Elizabethan-Sea-Dogs1 .html.
8. Quoted in Thomas, *The Slave Trade*, p. 21.
9. Quoted in Sheldon M. Stern, "It's Time to Face the Whole Truth About the Atlantic Slave Trade," George Mason University's History News Network, August 13, 2007. http://hnn .us/articles/41431.html#_edn10.
10. Quoted in Paul E. Lovejoy, *Trans-

formations in Slavery*. New York: Cambridge University Press, 2000, p. 33.
11. Quoted in Lovejoy, *Transformations in Slavery*, p. 42.
12. Quoted in Unesco, Lisbon, Portugal, International Conference, "The Ideology of Racial Hierarchy and the Construction of the European Slave Trade," December 1998. www.asante .net/articles/ideo-rac.html.

Chapter Two: The Infamous Triangular Trade

13. National Maritime Museum, "What Was the Triangular Trade?" www .nmm.ac.uk/freedom/viewTheme.cf m/theme/triangular.
14. National Archives, "British Transatlantic Slave Trade: Introduction." www.nationalarchives.gov.uk/catalo gue/rdleaflet.asp?sLeafletURL=http %3A%2F%2Fwww%2Enationalarchi ves%2Egov%2Euk%2Fcatalogue%2Fl eaflets%2Fri2076%2Ehtm&lBack=-1.
15. Quoted in PortCities Bristol, "Trade Goods: A Ship's Cargo for Africa." www.discoveringbristol.org.uk/sho wNarrative.php?sit_id=1&narId =9&nacId=12.
16. Quoted in Michael H. Cottman, *The Wreck of the Henrietta Marie*. New York: Harmony, 1999, pp. 70–71.
17. Quoted in Thomas, *The Slave Trade*, p. 363.

18. Quoted in Thomas, *The Slave Trade*, p. 364.
19. Quoted in Thomas, *The Slave Trade*, p. 374.
20. Quoted in Smithsonian Institution, *Captive Passage: The Transatlantic Slave Trade and the Making of the Americas.* Washington, DC: Smithsonian Institution Press, 2002, p. 59.
21. Quoted in Smithsonian Institution, *Captive Passage*, p. 75.
22. Quoted in Smithsonian Institution, *Captive Passage*, p. 53.

Chapter Three: Surviving the Middle Passage

23. Quoted in Cottman, *The Wreck of the Henrietta Marie*, p. 191.
24. Thomas, *The Slave Trade*, p. 408.
25. Quoted in Thomas, *The Slave Trade*, p. 415.
26. Quoted in Hanover College Department of History, "Olaudah Equiano, *The Interesting Narrative of the Life of Olaudah Equiano, or Gustavus Vassa, the African.*" http://history.hanover.edu/texts/Equiano/equiano_ch2_a.htm.
27. Quoted in Thomas, *The Slave Trade*, p. 420.
28. Equiano, *The Interesting Narrative of the Life of Olaudah Equiano*, p. 74.
29. Quoted in Smithsonian Institution, *Captive Passage*, pp. 68–69.
30. Quoted in Smithsonian Institution, *Captive Passage*, p. 70.
31. Quoted in Thomas, *The Slave Trade*, p. 418.
32. Quoted in Documenting the American South, "Narrative of the Enslavement of Ottobah Cugoano, a Native of Africa; Published by Himself, in the Year 1787." http://docsouth.unc.edu/neh/cugoano/cugoano.html.
33. Quoted in Smithsonian Institution, *Captive Passage*, p. 74.
34. Quoted in Hanover College Department of History, "Olaudah Equiano."
35. Quoted in Hanover College Department of History, "Olaudah Equiano."
36. Quoted in Hanover College Department of History, "Olaudah Equiano."
37. Thomas, *The Slave Trade*, p. 441.

Chapter Four: Because of the Slave Trade

38. Quoted in Kwesi Quartey, "Slavery: The Case for Reparations," *New African*, January 2008. http://findarticles.com/p/articles/mi_qa5391/is_200801/ai_n21301355/pg_1?tag=artBody;col1.
39. John Thornton, *Africa and Africans in the Making of the Atlantic World, 1400–1800*. Cambridge: Cambridge University Press, 1999, p. 152.
40. Cottman, *The Wreck of the Henrietta Marie*, p. 61.
41. Quoted in Cottman, *The Wreck of the Henrietta Marie*, pp. 62–63.
42. Quoted in Hanover College Department of History, "Olaudah Equiano."
43. Quoted in Hanover College Department of History, "Olaudah Equiano."
44. Quoted in Documenting the American South, "Venture Smith, *A Narrative of the Life and Adventures of Venture, a Native of Africa: But Resident Above Sixty Years in the United States of America. Related by Himself.*" http://docsouth.unc.edu/neh/venture/venture.html.
45. Quoted in Documenting the American South, "*Incidents in the Life of a Slave Girl.*

Written by Herself." http://docsouth.unc.edu/fpn/jacobs/jacobs.html.

46. Quoted in Documenting the American South, *"Incidents in the Life of a Slave Girl. Written by Herself."*

47. Quoted in Documenting the American South, *"Life of William Grimes, the Runaway Slave. Written by Himself."* http://docsouth.unc .edu/neh/grimes 25/grimes25.html.

48. Bob Corbett, "The Haitian Revolution of 1791–1803: Part One," Webster University, St. Louis, MO (http://www .webster.edu/~corbetre/haiti/history /revolution/revolution1.htm).

49. Simon Schama, *Rough Crossings: Britain, the Slaves, and the American Revolution.* New York: HarperCollins, 2006, p. 108.

50. Schama, *Rough Crossings*, pp. 11–12.

Chapter Five: "Am I Not a Man and a Brother?"

51. Quoted in Schama, *Rough Crossings*, pp. 158–59.

52. Quoted in Thomas, *The Slave Trade*, p. 489.

53. Quoted in Isabel Wolff, "How Did the Real Hero of the Anti-slavery Movement Get Airbrushed Out of History?" *Mail Online*, March 23, 2007. www.dailymail.co.uk/news/article-444105/How-did-real-hero-anti-slavery-movement-airbrushed-history .html.

54. Quoted in The Potteries, Stoke-on-Trent, England, "Did You Know? Josiah Wedgwood Was a Keen Advocate of the Slavery Abolition Movement." www.thepotteries.org/did _you /005.htm.

55. Quoted in Thomas, *The Slave Trade*, p. 510.

56. Quoted in Thomas, *The Slave Trade*, p. 510.

57. Quoted in Thomas, *The Slave Trade*, p. 494.

58. Quoted in Brycchan Carey, "William Wilberforce's 1789 Abolition Speech." www.brycchancarey.com/abolition/ wilberforce2.htm.

59. Quoted in Thomas, *The Slave Trade*, p. 508.

60. Quoted in Thomas, *The Slave Trade*, p. 508.

61. Quoted in Thomas, *The Slave Trade*, pp. 541–42.

62. Quoted in Thomas, *The Slave Trade*, p. 551.

63. Quoted in "Wilberforce and Slavery," Open University, UK. http://open learn.open.ac.uk/file.php/1582/A20 7_9_5.pdf.

64. Quoted in Thomas, *The Slave Trade*, p. 552.

Chapter Six: After the Abolition of the Slave Trade

65. Quoted in Thomas, *The Slave Trade*, p. 567.

66. Quoted in Thomas, *The Slave Trade*, p. 582.

67. Thomas, *The Slave Trade*, p. 591.

68. Quoted in Thomas, *The Slave Trade*, p. 596.

69. Quoted in Thomas, *The Slave Trade*, p. 688.

70. Quoted in Arthur Abraham, "AMISTAD REVOLT—An Historical Legacy of Sierra Leone and the United States," Amistad America. www.amistadamer ica.org/content/blogcategory/177/201.

71. Quoted in Abraham, "AMISTAD REVOLT."

72. Quoted in Abraham, "AMISTAD REVOLT."

73. Quoted in Amistad America, "Argument of John Quincy Adams, Before the Supreme Court of the United States." www.amistadamerica.org/component/option,com_wrapper/Itemid,96.

Chapter Seven: Transformed by the Slave Trade

74. W.E.B. Du Bois, *The Souls of Black Folk*. Chicago: McClurg, 1938, p. 3.
75. Thornton, *Africa and Africans in the Making of the Atlantic World*, p. 320.
76. Quoted in Dirk Kohnert, "Cultures of Innovation of the African Poor: Common Roots, Shared Traits, Joint Prospects? On the Articulation of Multiple Modernities in African Societies and Black Diasporas in Latin America," MPRA Paper No. 3704, July 2006, p. 26, German Institute of Global and Area Studies. http://mpra.ub.uni-muenchen.de/3704/11/MPRA_paper_3704.pdf.
77. Thornton, *Africa and Africans in the Making of the Atlantic World*, p. 320.
78. Jihan Abdalla, "Brazil's Black Guerrillas," Brazzil, March 2003. www.brazzil.com/p149mar03.htm.
79. Du Bois, *The Souls of Black Folk*, p. 255.
80. Du Bois, *The Souls of Black Folk*, pp. 250–51.
81. DuBois, *The Souls of Black Folk*, pp. 250–51.
82. Gerald Early, "Slavery: History in the Key of Jazz," Jazz: A Film by Ken Burns, PBS. www.pbs.org/jazz/time/time_slavery.htm.
83. Quoted in Smithsonian Institution, *Captive Passage*, p. 112.
84. Smithsonian Institution, *Captive Passage*, p. 11.
85. Thomas, *The Slave Trade*, p. 226.
86. Lovejoy, *Transformations in Slavery*, p. 66.
87. Quoted in Thornton, *Africa and Africans in the Making of the Atlantic World*, p. 308.
88. The Applied History Research Group, "4.5 The Impact of the Slave Trade," University of Calgary. www.ucalgary.ca/applied_history/tutor/migrations/four5.html.
89. Quoted in Cottman, *The Wreck of the Henrietta Marie*, p. 197.
90. John Henrik Clarke, "Education for a New Reality in the African World: The African Holocaust—the Slave Trade," part 3, AfricaWithin.Com. www.africawithin.com/clarke/part30f10.htm.
91. Quoted in "The Transatlantic Slave Trade, 1450–1750," p. 4, Thinkquest.org. http://library.thinkquest.org/13406/ta/4.htm.

For Further Reading

Books

Margarita Engle, *The Poet Slave of Cuba: A Biography of Juan Francisco Manzano*. New York: Holt, 2006. This beautiful award-winning book uses poetry to tell the true story of the life of the famous Cuban slave poet. It tells of the cruelties of his enslavement and the endurance of his spirit.

R.G. Grant, *The African-American Slave Trade*. Hauppauge, NY: Barron's Educational Series, 2003. Concentrating on the United States, this short book discusses Africans' journey to America and slave life as it was experienced by the people who endured it.

Anne Kamma and Pamela Johnson, *If You Lived When There Was Slavery in America*. New York: Scholastic, 2004. Everyday life as a slave in the United States is shown through the writings and oral histories of former slaves. Details about work, education, clothing, and family life are included.

Tim McNeese, *The Abolitionist Movement: Ending Slavery*. New York: Chelsea House, 2007. This is a detailed exploration of the crusade to end slavery in the United States, beginning at the time of the Revolutionary War and continuing through the Civil War and slavery's abolition.

Peter H. Wood, *Strange New Land: Africans in Colonial America*. New York: Oxford University Press, 2003. This book describes the earliest beginnings of the slave trade and slavery in North America, the lives of the African captives, and the earliest struggles for freedom.

Web Sites

The Atlantic Slave Trade and Slave Life in the Americas: A Visual Record (http://hitchcock.itc.virginia.edu/Slavery/index.php). This is a collection of more than a thousand images of the slave era. It is a project of the Virginia Foundation for the Humanities and the University of Virginia. Visitors can explore the collection and click the link "Slave Ships & the Atlantic Crossing" to see art and photo images of slave ships, manacles, and the conditions of the captives.

Slavery in America: Narratives/ Biographies (www.slaveryinamerica.org/narratives/overview.htm). This Web site is a compilation of stories and comments from people who lived when slavery existed in America.

Slaves' Stories, National Museums Liverpool (www.liverpoolmuseums.org.uk/nof/slavery). At this site from the Liverpool Museum in the United Kingdom, visitors can follow the ordeals of four different Africans captured and sold into slavery in the year 1780. The stories are composites of the kinds of people and experiences that were involved in the slave trade.

Triangular Trade, National Maritime Museum (www.nmm.ac.uk/freedom/viewTheme.cfm/theme/triangular). This British exhibit allows visitors to follow a ship's triangular trade route with a click of the mouse.

2007–2008 Amistad America (www.amistadamerica.org). Since 2007 a replica of the *Amistad* has been sailing North American waters as a real-life history exhibit. The history of the *Amistad* incident is explained in detail, and tour news is updated regularly.

The Wreck of the Henrietta Marie: A Slave Ship Speaks (www.melfisher.org/exhibitions/henriettamarie). In 1972 the wreck of the slaving ship *Henrietta Marie* was discovered on the ocean floor off Key West, Florida. The discovery led to years of research and diving expeditions. At the Mel Fisher Maritime Heritage Society Web site, visitors can see images of the artifacts found and learn the importance of this historical find.

Index

A
Abdalla, Jihan, 85
Adams, John, 57
Adams, John Quincy, 80–81
Africa
  colony for freed slaves in, 89
  first slave trading posts in, 18, 20
  slave trade and, 87–88, 90, 92
Africa (slave ship), 23–24
African culture, 83–85
African Diaspora, 92
The African Trade, the Great Pillar and Support of the British Plantation Trade in America (Postlethwayt), 45
Africans in America (TV series), 15
Age of Enlightenment, 9
Alves, Castro, 68
"Amazing Grace" (hymn), 41
American Colonization Society, 89
Amistad (slave ship) revolt, 77–81, *78–79*
Asientos, 24

B
Black Joke (slave ship), 73
Boukman (African priest), 84
Boyer, Jean-Pierre, 74
Brazil, 68, 71
  abolition of slave trade by, 72, 74
  as largest recipient of slaves, 32
  Maroons in, 53
  slaves retain African culture in, 85
British National Maritime Museum, 22
Brookes (slave ship), 33, 35

C
Campeadore (slave ship), 71
Capoeira (martial art), 85, *85*
Chamberlaine, Thomas, 30
Cidjoe (Maroon leader), 53
Cinque, Joseph. *See* Sengbe Pieh
Clarke, John Henrik, 92
Clarkson, Thomas, 60, 61–62, 63
Clay, Henry, 89
Collingwood, Luke, 58, 60
Columbus, Christopher, 13, *13*, 15
Committee for the Abolition of the Slave Trade, 60
Corbett, Bob, 53
Cottmann, Michael, 47
Cotton gin, 50, *50*
Cugoano, Ottobah, 40–41

D
Davis, David Brion, 17
Declaration of Independence, 55, 57
Denmark, 72
Dickens, Charles, 9
Dorothy (slave ship), 38
Du Bois, W.E.B., 82–83, 86
Duke of Cambridge (slave ship), 41

E
Early, Gerald, 86
Elizabeth I (English queen), 12
Equiano, Olaudah, 35, 42, *49*, 60
  life of, 47–48

F
Ferriers (slave ship), 41
Fox, Charles James, 66
France
  abolition of slavery by, 72
  legalization of slave trade in, 66
Franklin, Benjamin, 61

G
Gorée Island, 26, 33
Great Britain
  abolition of slave trade in, 66, 68, 72
Grenville, William, 63, 67, 68
Grimes, William, 53
Gullah culture, 91

H
Haiti (St. Dominigue)
  citizenship for blacks and, 74
  religion and African nations of, 84
  slave revolt in, 53, *54–55*, 55, 57
Hakluyt, Richard, 10
Hawkins, John, 10, *11*, 12
Henrietta Marie (slave ship), 25–26,
  30, 31, 47
Henry, Patrick, 57
Henry the Navigator (Portuguese
  monarch), 12, 13–15, *14*
Hispaniola, 10
  See also Haiti

I
Irby, Frederick, 70

Isabella I (Spanish queen), 15
Islamic empire, 20

J
Jacobs, Harriet, 51
Jefferson, Thomas, 68
Jones, Curtis, 83
Jordan, Winthrop, 21

K
Kali, 80
Kensal, James, 58

L
Labat, Jean-Baptiste, 47
Letter on the Abolition of the Slave Trade
  (Wilberforce), 66, 68
Liberia, 89
  freed slaves arriving in, *89*
Lovejoy, Paul E., 88

M
Maroons, 53
Merrick, George, 23, 24, 25
Middle Passage, 29–30, *37*
Montez, Pedro, 77–78
More, Hannah, 61
*Morning Chronicle and London Adver-
  tiser* (newspaper), 60

N
Nanny (Maroon leader), 53
Napoleon Bonaparte, 66, 68
Ndiaye, Joseph, 33, 92
New World colonies, 22
Newton, John, 41
North America
  importance of slavery in, 45–46,
  51

O

Oxford (slave ship), 38

P

Palmer, Colin A., 32
Phillips, John, 29
Pitt, William, 63
Polite, Thomalind, *56*
Portugal
    abolition of slave trade by, 72, 74
    and British Navy, 71–72
    European slave trade and, 12–15
    West African trading posts
        established by, 18, 20
Postlethwayt, Malachy, 45
Prince of Orange (slave ship), 31

R

Race, 21
Randolph, John, 89
Rawley, James A., 9
Revolutionary War, 55
Romilly, Samuel, 68
Royal African Company, 28
Ruiz, Jose, 77–78

S

São Joáo (slave ship), 70
São Tomé, 18, 20
Schama, Simon, 55
Sengbe Pieh (Joseph Cinque), *76,*
    77–78, 81
Sharp, Granville, 60, 63
Slave auctions, 42–43
    announcement of, *43*
Slave emancipation medallion, *62*
Slave factories, *25*, 26
Slave revolts
    in Haiti, *55–56*
    on slave ships, 40–42

See also Amistad revolt
Slave ships, 33, *34*, 35
    conditions/treatment of slave on,
        35–37, 38–40
    deaths on, 31, 38, 42
    revolts on, 40–42
    slaves in hold of, *36*
Slave trade. *See* Transatlantic slave
    trade
Slavery
    acceptance of, 8–9
    biblical justification for, 17
    early history of, 15–17
    in North America, 51
Slaves, *27*
    bearing scars of whippings, *52*
    Egyptian wall painting of, *16*
    in hold of slave ship, *36*
    impact of forced removal on, 82–83
    in Middle Passage, 37
    oral histories of, 87
    on slave ships, *39*
    smuggling of, 75, 76
    working cotton gin, *50*
Smith, Venture, 48–49
Society of Friends (Quakers), 60
Sorrow songs, 85–86
Spain
    abolition of slave trade by, 72, 74
    and British interference, 71–72
    licensing of slave traders by, 24
Sparke, John, 12
St. Dominigue. *See* Haiti (St. Dominigue)
Sugar plantations, 30, 46–47
    slaves on, *46*

T

Tattersfield, Nigel, 26
Taylor, John, 26
Tegesibu (African king), 26

Thomas, Hugh, 8, 37, 44, 73, 87
Thornton, John, 45, 83, 85, 90
Transatlantic slave trade
  abolition of, 72
  British, 67, 70-72
  impact on Africa, 82, 87–88, 90, 92
  movement to abolish, 60–63, 65–66
  triangle trade and, 22, 23, 31–32
  voyages during, 75
Triangle trade, 22, 23, 31–32

U
United States
  abolition of slavery by, 72
  ends participation in slave trade, 68
  Gullah culture in, 91
  importance of slavery in, 45–46
  persistence of slavery in, 72
  smuggling of slaves, 75, 77

V
Van Buren, Martin, 78
Voudou (Voodoo), 84

W
War of 1812, 72
Washington, George, 57
Wedgwood, Josiah, 60–61, 62
Wellington, Duke of, 73
Whitney, Eli, 50
Wilberforce, William, 61, 63, *64,*
  65–66, 68
Wilberforce (Haitian naval ship), 74
Wilson, Isaac, 35
Wollstonecraft, Mary, 61

Z
Zong (slave ship), 58–59
  replica of, *59*

Picture Credits

Cover, Hulton Archive Getty Images
© The London Art Archive/Alamy, 34
AP Images, 76
The Art Archive, 11
The Art Archive/Culver Pictures, 86
The Art Archive/Private Collection/Marc Charmet, 39
The Art Archive/Tokyo National Museum/Laurie Platt Winfrey, 6 (lower left)
Art Resource, NY, 19
HIP/Art Resource, NY, 6 (lower right)
Erich Lessing/Art Resource, NY, 13, 16
British Library, London, UK/© British Library Board. All Rights reserved./The
    Bridgeman Art Library, 46
Private Collection/The Bridgeman Art Library, 73
Private Collection/© Michael Graham-Stewart/The Bridgeman Art Library, 71
Private Collection/© Look and Learn/The Bridgeman Art Library, 88
© Wilberforce House, Hull City Museums and Art Galleries, UK/© DACS/The
    Bridgeman Art Library, 61
Photo by Rick McKee/charlestonphotographer.com, 56
© Bettmann/Corbis, 54–55
American School/The Bridgeman Art Library/Getty Images, 40
English School/The Bridgeman Art Library/Getty Images, 49
William Hackwood/The Bridgeman Art Library/Getty Images, 62
William Jackson/The Bridgeman Art Library/Getty Images, 67
After Eugene Antoine Samuel Lavieille/The Bridgeman Art Library/Getty
    Images, 7 (lower)
Gaston Melingue/The Bridgeman Art Library/Getty Images, 7 (upper)
John Rising/The Bridgeman Art Library/Getty Images, 64
Hulton Archive/Getty Images, 31
MPI/Hulton Archive/Getty Images, 29, 52, 78–79
Peter Macdiarmid/Getty Images, 59
Andre Penner/SambaPhoto/Getty Images, 85
Time Life Pictures/Mansell/Time Life Pictures/Getty Images, 27
Getty Images, 50
The Granger Collection, New York, 23, 89
The Library of Congress, 14, 25, 36, 43
The Picture Desk, Inc., 6 (upper)
© sandyjones.com, 91

About the Author

Toney Allman holds degrees from Ohio State University and the University of Hawaii. She currently lives in Virginia, where she enjoys a rural lifestyle and researches and writes for students. She has completed more than thirty nonfiction books on a variety of topics.